what it means
to be
avant-garde

also by david antin

autobiography (1967)

definitions (1967)

code of flag behavior (1968)

meditations (1971)

talking (1972)

after the war (1973)

talking at the boundaries (1976)

whos listening out there (1979)

tuning (1984)

Selected Poems: 1963–1973 (1991)

david antin

what it means
to be
avant-garde

a new directions book

Grateful acknowledgment is made to the editors and publishers of books and magazines in which much of the contents of this volume first appeared: *Formations, The Green American Tradition: Essays and Poems for Sherman Paul* (Baton Rouge: Louisiana State University Press, 1989), *High Performance, New Directions in Prose & Poetry* (nos. 50 and 52), *Representations*.

Manufactured in the United States of America
New Directions Books are printed on acid-free paper.
First published as New Directions Paperbook 760 in 1993
Published simultaneously in Canada by Penguin Books Canada Limited

Library of Congress Cataloging-in-Publication Data

Antin, David.
What it means to be avant-garde / David Antin.
p.   cm.
    ISBN 0–8112–1238–6
I. Title.
PS3551.N75W5   1993   93–9189
811'.54—dc20   CIP

New Directions Books are published for James Laughlin
by New Directions Publishing Corporation,
80 Eighth Avenue, New York 10011

contents

for peter and jeanette and mollie,

so long

Foreigners, because they never have enough words to express their ideas, often invent remarkable new modes of expression. Poets are all foreigners.

DENIS DIDEROT

what it means
to be
avant-garde

some time around the beginning of summer weba called me
and asked if i would be willing to read at lace in early
september   it was part of the l.a. festival and there would
be lots of things going on all over town and i'd be reading
with some other poet i'd never heard of was that all right?
    i said that was fine with me because there were lots of
poets i'd never heard of but i hoped she understood that i
dont read anymore i talk and that whatever i happened to say
    that was my poetry   which was a kind of performance
        and she let me know that was all right with her but she
wanted me to know they had very little money and could pay
me only two hundred dollars   and that was very little money
        but i live in san diego which is not very far from
downtown l.a. and i was feeling friendly toward lace as an
    alternate space that supported performance in a way that
the museums and other los angeles institutions do not   and
in spite of the fact that the very next day i would have to
fly to a performance in new york i said okay   and thats how
    i wound up on

the fringe

i hadnt been thinking about los angeles before coming up
here   it was merely that i was reading the los angeles
times   and the los angeles times is one of those newspapers
which like most big newspapers   has a sense of importance
to it   self importance   and the los angeles times is
partly characterized by this sense of self importance
     along with a considerable incompetence thats probably no
worse than that of most great newspapers   except that
you expect from its respectable pages and its massiveness
     most of it filled with ads   you expect from its
thickness and length that when it describes things it will
describe them with some accuracy
                                        this is a great mistake   i
     mean youre not supposed to believe whats in a newspaper
     youre supposed to be entertained by it   everybody knows
that

     if you have ever been at any event or anything that
could be described as a happening and it was reported
afterward in the newspapers   it was somehow always wrong
     this is a standard experience i was standing next to
their reporter and he got it all wrong   so i should be used
to it   but im not
                         and i started reading the calendar section
     and you cant really read the calendar section   all you
can do is look at it   usually i open the paper to the
sports section since i already know what the headlines are
going to say and i figure i'll wait because theyre kind of
grim   i'll read the real articles later   besides im going
to read the new york times to find out what happened a bit
more precisely   theyre a little bit more self important

but a little more accurate
                              so i turn to the calendar section
    to see if theyre reviewing anybody i know   and then i
realized i was part of the fringe and i thought that was
wonderful   i wondered what sort of fringe that was going to
    be   and i imagined some large prayer shawl with long
    tassels   or a tablecloth   or i imagined a room with the
kind of lighting where the center is brilliantly lit with the
    kind of lights i would have cut so that i wouldnt have them
    in my face   and there at the edge there was some sort of
diffraction fringe   and it occurred to me that maybe it
    wasnt such a good thing to be on the fringe   at least you
got the impression from the l.a. times that it wasnt
necessarily the best thing
                              i knew that they didnt think it was
really a good thing to be on the fringe   but they wanted to
    cheer us up if we were on it   because it was a los angeles
fringe and we were trying hard   they seemed to suggest that
    we might be here and there could be an agent out there who
might see us
                      is anybody here an agent?   no agents out there
    but if you cant get an agent at least you could raise
funding   there might be a director of some organization out
there that could help us get funding   i could raise lots
of funding so   i could talk   thats what i really need
    to raise lots of money to allow me to come and talk

                its very important to raise lots of money   not
because i talk better for money   and not even because i
talk worse for it   but that somehow the presence of the
money in a very attractive pile   over there   would make
    it seem so much more important when i started to talk
    because when i started to talk people out there would
evaluate the height of the pile of money   if there was a
huge pile of money over there then every one of my words
    would become extremely valuable   because everyone would
    count up the number of words and divide it into the number
of dollars in order to calculate how many dollars a word
i'm getting   thats what the l.a. times does in the sports
    section

        4

say for example a baseball player bats two eighty
and hits twenty home runs   when i was a kid you didnt know
how much money he made   so a guy who hit 280 and hit 20
home runs was a good ballplayer   they said he was okay
    nowadays if you hit 280 and 20 home runs youre a superstar
    now being a superstar has a new meaning   i used to
think somebody was a star   an astronomical judgment
    but i thought they were players like stan musial or pete
reiser   they won batting championships they hit 350 or
    like hank greenberg or mickey mantle they hit forty home
    runs and they were stars   but you didnt figure out how
many dollars they got for each swing   in those days you
    couldnt say mickey mantle is making twenty-five hundred
dollars per at bat and thats why he's a superstar   a star
of the first magnitude
                    now we have a whole family of
    astronomical categories   you have whole classes of stars
and superstars   a star of the first magnitude   a white
    giant a red dwarf   and the way you calibrate it is you
look to see how much money he makes and divide it into his
number of at bats   if he's a superstar who sits on the
bench a lot and doesnt come up to bat enough   maybe you
    figure out how much he's making a day   and of course the
l.a. times publishes a scorecard   who's making the most
    money   that is of all the people who are most obnoxious in
current contemporary culture the question is who is making
    the most money   eddie murphy or some other jerk?
    now i confess to no enthusiasm for the people who
are usually in the white light or the center of the
    tablecloth   and this of course causes a bit of a problem
because im coming up to be in the fringe but i dont want to
    get into the white light   would i be in the japanese
cultural center?   i dont speak japanese i dont want to
    speak japanese   although i like the idea of other people
speaking it   i think its a nice sounding language but its
not one of mine   i have others but not japanese   but most
    people going to the japanese cultural center are not
speaking japanese theyre doing some kind of dance   theyre
    spinning around like dervishes or doing something important
    with trapezes or telling jokes

but i dont even tell jokes not really   if i told
jokes they could say how much money i got for a joke   but
i realized i like the fringe   because im used to it   in
a certain sense ive always felt i was in the right place
     and the right place was a place shaded from the bright
light at the center of the tablecloth   and i liked living
there   it seemed to be the place where everything
meaningful happened   but thats because i didnt read the
los angeles times   with sufficient assiduity to learn from
it
     the los angeles times is rather wonderful   weba   when
she was organizing this series of performances asked me to
call somebody at the los angeles times   and i was kind of
absent minded and she said call at 4:30   this woman
     janice something or other i dont remember her name
     but i said all right i dont mind calling somebody at
the los angeles times   they want to interview you she said
     so i wrote myself a note somewhere reminding me to call
janice somebody or other at the los angeles times at 4:30
     but then weba called back an hour later and said no
     can you call her at 5:00   and i figured if i could call
her at 4:30 i could just as easily call her at 5:00
     because i'll be working at my word processor or drinking
a cup of coffee   so its nothing to me and i put down call
her at five
            now when somebody says to me do something at five
i figure they mean somewhere in the reasonable range of five
     and this was an interesting experience   i called this
woman at five minutes afer five and she says   "i wish you
had called at five"   i say "oh?"   and she says "i have
someone calling at 5:15"   i said "well youre not going to
learn very much talking to me for ten minutes   because what
i do is probably going to be completely incomprehensible to
     you"   she said "well if you dont want me to interview
you..."   i said "i dont really give a damn" and hung up

            now i know that i had confused her   because she'd
figured that i would surely get an agent if she put me in the
paper   i would get a contract to do what i do   at clubs
     in fullerton   in glendale   in eagle rock   thats

terrific   i could go and entertain people in eagle rock
and be in the minor leagues and gradually work my way up to
the mark taper   or the japanese cultural center   and get
a film contract   wow i would be a talking animal   on
film   a poet on film   or maybe a talking animal on a
sitcom or in a scene in a police story where theyve got a
space they have to fill with a performance artist because
what they always do is even too boring for them   the
way they have some performance artist come and do the
heavy
        theres a new york performance artist who's a sort of
mediocre melodramatic actor named bogosian   he's not
terrible he's all right   he's a perfectly adequate
ordinary performance artist   but all his life he wants to
be an actor on tv and do police shows   and this is his
chance
        but i couldnt do that   i dont want to do police
shows   i despise actors and i can only look at police shows
for the first 10 minutes   so i realized i didnt have this
right   and i asked myself how do i get this right   i dont
want to be a success   and ive succeeded   theres an
ambiguity about not wanting to be a success
                                    i wanted to be a
poet   when you say you want to be a poet you already know
that you dont want to be a success   the model for poetry is
not to be a success   thats the first model you learn
    the first ones went blind   later they died of
tuberculosis or committed suicide or drowned   when i was a
kid i remember there was a big book containing all the poems
of keats and shelley   they were both great poets and they
both died young   one got tuberculosis and the other
couldnt swim   and these were intense serious people who
didnt want to make it into the white light as long as
they were alive   or so the story went   and they didnt
want to succeed because they were fringe types   poets

and if thats what you wanted to be you figured out how
to get tuberculosis   but i was too healthy i was a jock   i
couldnt get tuberculosis i wasnt the type   but i could
do something dangerous and fall off a cliff   i had an uncle

who fell off a cliff

                         he was my favorite uncle   i didnt
know him very long   he fell off a cliff shortly after i
got to know him   that was when i was very young   and i
was living with my grandmother and about twelve aunts   and
he was never around much he was always travelling and
being and doing something exciting somewhere else far away
from our quiet little house in brooklyn   sometimes he was
off organizing a union or being a steward on a yacht in
the south pacific or doing something mysterious in the
everglades

one time he returned with a very beautiful dark lady
with plumes   this was in the 1930s and i was a very little
kid   but i remember she looked wonderfully tall and
majestic in her plumes   trailing a feather boa that reached
all the way to the floor   and she was so tall and noble
looking that my aunt bette said she was an indian princess
and i didnt know much about india or princesses but i
supposed thats what an indian princess would have to look
like   a tall noble dark lady   gracious and beautiful
beyond belief

            and then they went away   later we heard that my
uncle was climbing the rockies and fell off a cliff and died
and that was my image of what a poet does   he doesnt
succeed   he takes odd jobs that are not good enough but
interesting   he goes and comes a lot and returns with
an indian princess before he finally disappears

            and while i didnt live like that   that was my
image of a poet   and i always lived in the way of being a
poet   which meant living the life of an artist   and when
i was a kid artists didnt drive rolls royces   and i didnt
know a single artist who had a rolls royce   i admit it was
a long time ago   it was in the fifties when i was in
college   i met a few artists and they had ratty looking
studios and made big paintings and didnt make lots of money
and some of them made very good paintings   some of them
        and some of them made very good sculpture   and not one
of them talked about money   i guess they were also still

living on the fringe

in the sixties they stopped living on the fringe
and moved to long island and lived in airy houses   but they
still had this idea of living on a fringe   maybe because
they had lived in cold water flats   or maybe they just
tried to live with that image because they thought that was
the way an artist was supposed to live   even after he
became rich   thats possible   but some time around the end
of the seventies the image changed   if you were going to
be an artist you were not supposed to be on the fringe
you were supposed to be twelve and a genius and know all
the rich people and make lots of paintings that would all
sell for fabulous amounts of money and travel around in a limousine
and then everybody would know you were an artist who was doing the
right thing   but that wasnt my life

as soon as i got out of college i found myself a cold
water flat   because that was what i was supposed to do
and its true that i wasnt poor because i was a technically
trained kid who could work at technical jobs or translating
jobs and make quite enough money to survive   but the one
thing i couldnt do because i didnt want to do it was to be
in the white light   it would have been a problem for me
anyway   the white light   what would the white light be
for somebody like me?   to get an important job with a big
corporation where theyre in the white light?   how do you
get into a big corporation?

first of all as soon as anyone says big
corporation i get sick to my stomach   i didnt want to work
for a big corporation   but somebody suggested that i try to
get a job at bell labs   i had done a lot of technical work
of various sorts and i had a kind of elaborate science
education   and it seemed plausible for me to go for this
job where i would have been a kind of communicator in this
great research oriented corporation between their scientists
who couldnt communicate anything to anyone in english
and the clever but uneducated people in that corporation
who would have turned that science into money

so i got an interview   i didnt really go to this

9

interview with any great enthusiasm   because up till then
i had been free lancing for a number of translating companies
    translating technical papers on french tranquilizers or
russian automation systems and various other pieces of
intellectual rubble i got paid well for and cared nothing
about   as long as i had enough free time to stay home and
write   but somebody got me this interview   and i agreed
    to go   i dont know why

        i guess it was a little like reading the l.a. times
and realizing they were sending me out into the white light
and this was my chance to get out of the fringe   but i had
this bad feeling about it
                        still i had a job hunting suit
    it was my one suit a very expensive suit   it was an
english tweed suit from which i still have the jacket   the
kind of tweed they dont make anymore   i took it to get it
repaired about three years ago because it had a moth hole in
    it   i took it to this italian tailor and he nearly fainted
when he saw the tweed   my god he said they dont make them
    like this anymore   now i teach at the university of
california   and this jacket is older than my oldest
graduate student and will probably be given as an inheritance
to my son   who's about the same size as i am   and he will
    probably pass it on to his son   if he has one   or to his
    daughter   and she'd probably look good in it if she was
    big enough   but this jacket was part of a suit the pants
of which have disappeared   they were big and floppy in a
fifties style i never liked and didnt realize would come back
again   but in those days this was my job hunting suit

        so i took my suit and went to meet these guys from
bell labs who were going to interview me   there were two of
    them   and they took me to a steak house over on greenwich
avenue   and i guess it would have been all right but you
    had to meet these guys to believe what they were like
        these were corporate men they werent scientists   who
later i got to know   queer germans and freaky swedes   but
these were profoundly middle american corporate men from some
place like cleveland or dubuque   and these corporate men
    took me to lunch

    10

          now how can i describe these corporate men
     they wore pale suits and had pale eyes and short well
brushed hair and wore tie pins and had neatly clipped nails
     and they had close shaves and dull shines on their
pebble grained shoes and their shirt sleeves extended
exactly one quarter of an inch below their suit sleeves
     and each one had a wrist watch with a gold metal band
     and i had known it was going to be like this so i had
loosened my tie and unbuttoned the collar of my shirt before
i saw them just to let them know that i was a little defiant
     about the white light

          and i took myself into the white light there and
     sat down with them and we talked for a while   and it was
a sort of technical talk about klystron tubes and computers
but it was more about making conversation   and every word
     that came from their middle american mouths made me
     feel that maybe the white light was the worst place to be
          i began to think white light   white light was maybe
like white bread   tiptop bread   which was an advertising
euphemism for low down dreg bread   or nonbread or foamed
     cardboard that just looked like bread   and tiptop bread
     was what they looked like the two corporate men   and i
     kept seeing tiptop bread as i looked into both their faces
     so white and polite and unperturbed   that i saw
tiptop tip top   and i began to believe that those were
     their names   tip and top
                              and that was very dangerous
     because when one of them would ask me a question i
would ask myself is this one tip or top and almost forgot
     to answer the question   and it was getting me very buggy
because it reminded me that i had two goldfish once when i
was a kid   and i'd named one of them mike and the other
     one sam   but they swam around in the same bowl and they
looked so much alike that i was never sure which was mike
and which was sam
                    and i was a kid about five and i thought i
     was supposed to love my pets   but i was never sure when i
talked to sam that it wasnt mike or   when i talked to mike
     it wasnt sam   and this made me feel bad   because i might

                                             11

look sincerely into the fishbowl and say "sam   look sam
i'm having a lot of trouble in school   they keep wanting me
  to do things i dont want to do"   and then i would think
maybe im talking to mike
                            and i knew all along i might be
talking to mike instead of to sam   and that didnt feel
right   it felt insincere   because instead of talking with
heartfelt sorrow to my own pet that i knew was listening
   it was like i didnt care   and no matter how full of
conviction i was when i said sam   i would always know that
it might be mike
                      and it was like i didnt care   because
someone who really loved his goldfish would have been able to
distinguish the special flecks on his belly or the shape of
  his little flipper and would have known that this was mike
and this was sam   but i just cared enough to feed them
  and talk to them occasionally when i was alone in the house
with my first grade problems

          and here were mike and sam all over again   and i
was sitting with them having lunch   and i started feeling
  guilty all over again   and i said to myself how am i ever
going to get into the white light and out of the fringe
     these are the janissaries who stand by the bright lit
gate   the two guards who stand between me and the luminous
  corporate life of bell labs   and i will just have to talk
  to these people and pretend that i know their names and can
    tell them apart
                        and i proceeded to talk a blue streak
because i figured that if i did most of the talking i didnt
  have to remember their names or what each one had said
   and so we talked about klystron tubes and that was safe
and conservative type talk because it was a conventional
   technology and easy to talk to white bread about since it
didnt involve anybodys point of view   but it couldnt go
   very far either and so i pushed the conversation into
computers   which was better because they were new enough
    then for everybody to have something to say about them that
wasnt serious   but in my exhilaration at being able to
keep talking and not having to deal with my problems with

tip and top i started in on biological computers and before
i knew it i was fantasizing about how small a computer you
could make if all of its memory system was made of yeasts
or little bacteria   and how you could cultivate them
       so that inputting information into them would be like a
kind of microfarming if it was yeast or like a kind of
ranching if it was little cocci that you could round up to
get the cellular information out of   and maybe using some
kind of isotope tracer system to read the information   or
feeding them with dyes to get a read out with some kind of
laser technology   and then i began to worry about
mutations
               you'd have all this information coded into their
cellular material   but what if they started mutating   and
i worried about this for a while but then it occurred to me
that might be a good thing   because so far the main problem
with computers was the mechanical nature of their memories
   and here was a chance to introduce a kind of organic
randomness into the system   which was maybe more like human
memory after all   and i thought it sounded like a great
 idea
       but then i looked into the faces of the two corporate
men sitting across from me and i realized i had gone too far
   i looked into tips freckled slightly reddish face and i
saw that it was blank while top was brooding somberly over
his martini   or maybe it was the other way around   and i
remembered these werent even scientists they were just two
 ex-engineers now in middle management   and why was i
wasting my time talking to them about filing information
among amino acids   but i wouldnt let up

          i said you could print a bible there   it would be
a first in sacred agriculture   you would make scripture on
the head of a pin seem spendthrift of space   because you
could reduce the memory bank to the size of a colony of
microbes or a family of viruses   and i figured that half
the worlds knowledge could be transmitted in somebodys sneeze
       and i knew this was not a good idea   i should have
been talking with them about german patents   because i had
been running a seedy american wing of an international

scientific publishing company that translated german patents
and that was a place that wasnt in the white light

it was in a shabby little manhattan office
building on east twenty-third street close to fourth avenue
and our parent outfit was a more glamorous international
company run by an english science hustler who was really
a czech science hustler who had bought up this little
american scientific translation company on twenty-third
street along with a chi-chi looking carriage trade bookstore
further up the east side

he had set up these american organizations it seemed
to move money back and forth more freely across the atlantic
the way he moved it around europe   he owned a nearly
extinct high class publishing company in france and had
printing plants in poland he had acquired somehow by buying
up somebodys war indemnities and a castle in surrey that he
only had to pay the upkeep on because it was a national
monument and he seemed to have acquired our little
translating company with the aim of losing a reasonable
amount of money in a respectable way

so that this was not a
place in the white light and i could work there comfortably
like the hungarian vice president and the swiss comptroller
who i knew was really czech or at least he had a czech name
though he may have had swiss citizenship   and the only
mistake i ever made working for them was to make them an
awful lot of money in a surprising way   by getting them
to publish a translation of a german book on a new kind of
fuel cell electrode that could separate hydrogen from water
so that the fuel cell could run on it   and i wrote the
promo for it in such a way that it scared all the oil
companies into buying dozens of copies that i printed
cheaply like a special report which we sold at a hundred and
fifty bucks a shot

this caused us a lot of trouble because now we had all
this money coming in that we had to find some way of losing
since all this time we were supposed to be a write off
and they were very upset but this was all news to me

14

because if i knew they had wanted to lose money i could
have started a poetry magazine or backed an off-broadway show
i could have found lots of entertaining ways to lose money
      i could have opened an art gallery   but i guess they
wanted to lose money in a businesslike way   they didnt want
         to be in the white light either   they wanted to be
in a grey businesslike light that would mute their pretty
lurid operations   so they were also in the fringe and the
kind of international hustlers i could comfortably work for
because they made sense

            but there i was facing tip and top and   tip and
top and i werent getting along so well   because they didnt
   make sense to me and i knew i wasnt making sense to them
   as i raved on and on about the future of my little bacterial
   computers and looked into their glazed eyes knowing that
   you dont talk to white bread in a positive way about mould
      so i began to drink   first i ordered one manhattan and
then another   and then i did what everyone out on an
interview lunch knows youre not supposed to do
                                             interview lunch
is a little like a first date and you know that if they take
you to an expensive expense account restaurant youre not
supposed to order the most expensive dish on the menu   but
i went for the prime ribs anyway and i saw the shocked look
on the pallid redhead's face and the stolid dark one's glazed
nictating stare   and i said to myself this isnt what you
do when your out with white bread on the companys books in
the white light   this is not a problem in the fringe
      but i said fuck it and fuck you tip and top or top and
tip   whichever the case may be   and i kissed the job
goodbye and had four manhattans and ordered the rare prime
ribs au jus and the stuffed artichokes and all sorts of
   extras as tip and top began to look indigestive   because
i figured it should at least cost them for taking me out to
lunch and wasting my time because i would never see them
again

            and this is what happened   you could tell that i
wasnt suited for the light   that i was perfectly suited to
   the fringe that i lived on in a quite comfortable way   i

15

had a manhattan apartment with three rooms and a view of the
palisades that i had bought from somebody else in 1957 for
two hundred and fifty dollars   on which i paid eighteen
dollars and fifty cents a month rent   i could smell real
bread from the italian bakery across the street browse for
books in a good used bookstore in the next building   i had
a fireplace and gas heat and a john i shared in the hall
    and it cost me eighteen dollars and fifty cents a month
after i paid a fifteen percent increase   and it was a
great place to live even though the floor was slightly
slanted from the fireplace to the door and the bathroom was
out in the hall   but i shared it with an attractive blonde
who had the apartment across the way   and i thought it was
quite comfortable and that was the way to live   the way
poets were supposed to live

    or thats what i thought   because in those days i had
not seen the los angeles times   so i didnt know how people
should live   i didnt know i needed a ferrari   in fact i
wouldnt have known how to drive one   can you believe that?
    in los angeles?
                    this is a performance and some place
in a performance there always comes a time for confession
    well this is confession time and im confessing   in new
york in 1957 i was twenty-five years old and i didnt know
how to drive   or thats not really true   but i didnt know
how to drive a shift car and i didnt learn how to drive till
i was twenty
                and for los angeles thats amazing   in los
angeles how could you not learn how to drive at the age of
eleven?   everybody who drives here drives like somebody
who's eleven   in los angeles i figure theyre trying out
their eleven year old sensibilities on the road   and theyre
using their cap pistols and people get shot   but thats the
way it is in los angeles   you start early aiming for your
ferrari   and at the other guys ferrari if he's in your way

        i did buy a car in new york in 1957   but i had to
buy a poets car so i went around the city looking for one
    but what was a poets car?   i finally bought one out
of a backyard in queens from a sleazy looking polish guy who

16

sold it to me very cheap   it was an old sunbeam talbot
    an english car   a four seater with a convertible top
    and the reason it was so cheap was that its gear shift
was put in backwards   and i thought that was great because
  i had to park it in the street and i figured that way
nobody'd be able to steal it   a thief would jump the
    ignition get in the car and put it into forward and the
car would shoot backward and slam into the car behind it   i
  figured that ought to be enough to unnerve anyone but a real
professional
                everything was completely ass backwards in that
car or else completely eccentric   it had the longest clutch
  disengagement in the world   and if you didnt push far
enough on the clutch pedal you could be partially engaged
    and in different degrees of engagement all the way to the
end   so when i got used to it it seemed like the car had
  infinite gearing   you could be half in a gear or a quarter
or an eighth   which was marvelous in traffic after you got
  used to it and it really saved on gas and on your brakes
    but you needed a complete new set of driving reflexes
to drive that car
                but that was easy for me because i had
never driven a shift car before   all i'd ever driven was a
clunky plymouth with fluid drive   so what difference did it
  make to me that the gear shift was in backwards   my
sunbeam only cost me a few hundred dollars   and then it
  cost the rest of my money trying to fix it up so it would
work

        but there i was living in this perfectly reasonable
shabby human light   translating as little as i had to to
survive   writing poems going to poetry readings   and going
  to the theater   poetry readings were free and the theater
was cheap   even broadway which was a place i seldom went to
  because most of the time it had terrible plays and seats
that were cheap   and there was much better theater downtown
  where all of the seats were cheap   and then i could drive
    out to the country in my sunbeam talbot because gas was
  cheap   so you could live very cheaply if you didnt mind
living on the fringe   the fringe was cozy   all of these

nice things were going on and it was like being in their
shade   i had it made in the shade

still   while i was enjoying all this i couldnt
completely escape the sense that out there somewhere was the
bright light even if i didnt want to be in it   in the
united states you cant escape the sense that somebody thinks
you should not really be in the shade but out there in the
white light   maybe making a salary in six figures doing
things that everybody would have to see

now i had no need for a salary in six figures i only
paid eighteen dollars and seventy five cents a month rent
i could walk to a job that i went into at 10 o'clock in
the morning   this company that i managed   i used to walk
from west fourth street up to twenty-third street go for a
swim at the y   have a couple of cups of coffee and two
whole wheat doughnuts at chock-full-o-nuts   then walk
across town to my office   where maybe i would edit a
translation from some technical journal   read through a
couple of articles on a subject i was researching and then
walk over to fourth avenue to join my friend paul blackburn
who was editing an encyclopedia   for lunch in a
little german delicatessen on second avenue   then i might
go to the engineering library to look up a couple of things
or maybe translate an article and go home

and since i managed
this company i could do some of my work at home and i didnt
have to go in every day   there were days i could knock off
in the afternoon and go to the park or go visit my friends
who had a poetry cooperative on second avenue and east 10th
street called the blue yak

it was a poetry bookstore owned by
about ten poets i was one of them   and it never had any
books in it that werent poetry books   and we wanted it that
way   and it seemed we had all the reasonably interesting
american poetry books in there and nothing else   and we
didnt sell a lot of books but we didnt care   when nobody
came into the store we played yak ball with a plastic bat and
a great wad of rolled up newspaper   and you got a home run
if you hit it over the shelving   the only people who seemed

18

to come in were other poets or artists from the 10th street
galleries   except for a few curious tourists and a lot of
drunks who wandered in off the bowery
                                    we had a lot of
ukrainian drunks because just to the south and the east was
a ukrainian and polish neighborhood   and the ukrainian
drunks used to come in and scold us for just selling poetry
and not making any money   "vat you do you foolish kids
     you sell poetry you never make money never be success
you be like us   bums"   but how can you tell a drunken bum
you dont want to be a success   he knows better   he knows
you're supposed to be a success   he says you should put in
popular literature   readers digest   i say i dont read
readers digest   he says "not for you   for them"   he
knew we should be ashamed of ourselves for being on the
fringe   because he was there with us and he knew that he
was just a lousy bum   he thought "you dont want to be
lousy bum   you well brought up smart poets   get out of
here into light"

     but i suppose we never took this lesson sufficiently to
heart   though you might ask me "havent you ever really
wanted to be in the light?"   its a question ive asked
myself from time to time   and i dont think i really have
     but i sometimes feel guilty about it   when i ask the question
about not wanting what everybody else wants
                                        because
there used to be a lot of us   but now there are very few
and sometimes i think its just me   and sometimes i worry
what am i different from everybody else   stuck up   and
i worry   could they all be wrong?   and sometimes i feel
guilty about it   not wanting to be in the light   its not
giving the light a break   give the light a chance

          once i remember having it thrust upon us   it was
an accident   during the vietnamese war   now this wasnt
a light that we wanted   but the war was such a stupid
brutal business and there was no way of ignoring it or its
stupidity and brutality   because everyone in the light was
lying to us about it   when he was being elected   kennedy
had stood up there in the light and promised it to us   and

19

then he delivered it to us   and johnson went even better
on those promises   and there were a lot of us poets and
painters and sculptors who had gotten very angry about this
and we put together kinds of protests like a lot of other
people who were not artists

this was in the early days of
the war   around 1965   and because we were poets and
artists we organized readings and exhibitions against the
war   but because we were poets and artists these were
still fringe operations because they werent big enough to
get into the light   where all of kennedys and johnsons
boys dean rusk and mcnamara were telling their lies   and i
guess thats what david halberstam meant when he called them
the best and the brightest   that they were out there in
the light that was nearly blinding   their reflected light
was nearly blinding us   and the direct light was surely
blinding them   and thats how i now understand what
halberstam meant by the brightest   they were the people
who were hit by such bright light they were blinded by it
the way actors can be blinded by lights that come up and hit
them in the face so they cant see the audience   and i
suppose they wanted so much to be in the light that they
didnt mind being blinded by it or were used to it   and
didnt think like poets or performance artists that you had to
look at the audience to know what you were doing

but this wasnt the light we wanted   if you have
the light in your face its hard to see what youre doing
you have to act by rote   you make gestures based on
previous gestures that you've prepared in a mirror or a
monitor   and you cant see anybody but they can see you
i think the outcome of being in the light is that you
can hardly see anybody   and these guys were running a
government based on being in the light   being a government
in the light a country in the light   and every one of
those guys was a star of the first magnitude   though maybe
a lot more like a moon   the way they were having the light
hit them in the face

and you had the kennedys like the three bears   the
old fascist father   the big kennedy the little kennedy and

20

the littlest kennedy   and they had everything going for
them   the boys of promise lit unbelievably   the electric
companies were giving them the works   and there they were
in vietnam giving everybody else the works   sometimes i
think that the napalm they dropped was a function of this
love of the light   that all this fire was based on a fear
of the dark   what they wanted to do was turn on the lights
for all these dark little people who lived on the fringe so
they could see how great it was to be in the light

                                                all   those
scroungy little dark people living in the shade of those
little conical hats   crawling around in the jungles   what
we have to do is light up the jungles drop flares on them
        lets take a look at these people so we can see them in
the light and they dont have to live in the shade   if they
have lots of light theyll come and live like us   in
compounds   it will be wonderful we'll have bright lights
on their compounds like in stalag 17   because in all these
prison camps you have these great lights flooding the central
space and you can get right out there where they have all
the sights trained on you   and i thought that was what was
coming
            and thats when we all started protesting   and
protesting is a boring activity   its very boring   what
usually happens is you excite all of the people who agree
with you   and they all turn out to march with you   and
theres a kind of solidarity thats quite nice but really
boring   and if there are enough of you   you excite all
of the people who violently disagree with you and thats a
little more interesting but not much   its about as
interesting as a play by arthur miller   in which somebody
says yes and somebody says no and then they say it over and
over again only louder   and that was the way with a lot of the
protests   there were the marches   and all of the people
who were against the war marched in the middle of the
street   and all of the people who were against being
against the war lined up on the sidewalk   but when you
added them together they made up about one percent of the
people
            and the other ninety-nine percent dont give a damn

                                                            21

and that ninety-nine percent dont live in the light but
they dont live in the fringe either   they live in some kind
of penumbra out of which they contentedly look into the
    light   but we lived in the fringe and we came out
something like termites   and at first we marched or really
walked and that was nice but pious and boring   and lots of
us thought we should do something more interesting   so we
organized readings and held them in places where mostly
people who agreed with us came to hear them   and that was only
a little more interesting
                              and then some artists got together
and painted a van for us and the poets read poems out in the
street and that was a little more interesting but not much
    because everybody read poems about how bad the war was
or how bad those bright people were who were making the war
    or how bad we all felt about it   and the people who
wanted to hear that liked it and cheered and the people who
    didnt jeered or tried to shout us down   but it didnt
change anybodys mind about anything
                                        so i got the idea that
maybe we should take the van out to red hook or canarsie or
some place where we knew that everybody was for the war
    and we could defend it   we would show them photographs
of napalmed children and executed vietcong prisoners and
point out how in the higher scheme of things   if you threw
enough light on them these things were necessary and good
    and i figured if we threw enough light on enough of our
doings in vietnam we could even make these brooklyn italians
nauseous enough to chase us out of their neighborhoods
    and a lot of people thought this was a pretty good idea
but nobody had the heart for it   and it even made me a
little sick
            but we got the idea of holding a very big reading
in a huge place in which all the poets could read and to
which thousands of people could come to express their disgust
with the war   and we found the fillmore east   a huge
    barn of a place   a rock palace that could hold a couple
of thousand people   and it got donated to us so everybody
    could come for free   and thats how we got thrown into the
white light

22

because now that we had this huge barn of a place
we had to figure out how to get all those people into it we
had to advertise and we had to decide whether to charge
money for it to raise funds for other protests   but we
decided it should be free or nearly free   we thought it
should cost something that was nearly nothing because we
wanted a peoples reading to which anybody could come   and
we thought of bertolt brechts three-penny opera and decided
to charge everybody three cents   which was as close to
nothing as anything could get   and we called it the
three-penny poets reading against the war

and we got a lot of publicity out of that   from the
village voice and wbai   new yorks pacifica station   and
just as if we were in the white light we started thinking
about what would publicize this reading   and we figured
that we had every non-academic poet who happened to be in
new york and wanted to read against the war in that reading
including of course allen ginsberg   who was always part of
these things   and gregory corso   and bob creeley   who
happened to be in the city and wasnt always part of these
things   and even john ashbery who was never part of these
things and wasnt even sure that he was against the war   but
he lived in yorkville and when he saw some of his german
fascist neighbors put on a pro vietnam war rally he got so
disgusted at the sight of them he decided to read with us too

then somebody got the idea that because andrei
voznesensky was in town he ought to read with us   the idea
was that here he was in new york reading up at town hall
with the group of stuffed owls that hung around the american
academy of poets and he wasnt saying a thing against the war
and i'll admit this didnt make a lot of sense to me
because the soviet union had a specific stake in the war
like the united states and was backing the north vietnamese
government   and was naturally against the american backed
government of south vietnam   so it didnt seem that his
coming out against the american involvement was anything like
ours   because we werent backing any government   and we
were opposing our own government   and that was our business

23

but that was my opinion and nobody else's and   besides
voznesensky was a figure out of the bright light   a star
of the first magnitude and a bit of a novelty   and that
would mean a big draw   and since we were figuring like
the rest of those people in the white light a meeting was
arranged that took place for some reason or other in arthur
miller's suite in the hotel chelsea   and because i was one
of the organizers i got taken along   it was back in the
sixties and voznesensky was a cool guy   young and dark
and catlike   and sitting there in a his brand new cable
knit sweater from sweden or denmark or finland that must
have cost a thousand dollars he looked like a hipper
version of jean claude killy   he was clearly a guy in the
  white light

          now he was not a poet whose work i liked   in
english it sounded massively mediocre   and on the page in
the russian it didnt look an awful lot better   but i make
it a practice not to pass serious judgment on poets who
work under such different conditions from mine   and the
conditions he worked under were very different from mine
  he was a poet who worked under the white light   and
those poets who worked in the white light of red russia
                                        i dont
like to use the word red for russia really   i dont like to
use the word communist for russia   if i were a communist
   which im not   i would be appalled to identify russia
with communism   i would regard russia as the worst example
   of appropriation   of a term that once had some decent
human significance and turning it into a mean spirited
bureaucratic disaster   but thats theyre problem and not
  being a communist its not mine
                         but here we were meeting with
one of these celebrity poets from the russian bureaucracy
    and he's one of these poets who read in stadiums over
loudspeaker systems to thousands of happy workers while we
read in human voices to a rooomful   he's like a soccer
hero or an olympic skier or a chess champion a public figure
    and my friends are hassling with him here at the chelsea
about why he should make some kind of statement by reading

with us at the fillmore

and he's a cool guy who's used to the white light
and the way i see it understands english well enough to
make up his mind to answer us directly   but he has an
interpreter by his side   which means a security agent and
he listens to what we say and then he listens to this guy
interpret it   which means he has two chances to listen to
what we have to say   and this gives him time enough to
think   and he probably has to think hard because decisions
they make in the white light are really visible   because
who knows what russia's interests in vietnam really are

all along russia has been supplying the north
vietnamese government   though sometimes denying this   and
one reason theyre backing north vietnam is that china's
opposing it   so the soviet union's support for north
vietnam is related to their quarrel with china as much as their
support for socialism or their opposition to the united
states   and who knows what impression the soviet union
wants one of their star official poets to put out when he's
on a cultural tour in the white light of the united states
and who knows what impression this not always so docile
star wants to put out himself
it's all very interesting but not very readable
though in a few days he calls to tell us he will read
with us   and by this time the reading is very much in the
white light   marlene dietrich has agreed to m.c. for us
i admit i loved that   the idea of being introduced by
marlene dietrich   maybe i didnt care much for the white
light and andrei voznesensky but i loved the idea of marlene
dietrich
and we go on the bob fass show on wbai and plug
the three-penny poets reading against the war in vietnam
that will feature andrei voznesensky reading with his
american anti-war colleagues and marlene dietrich as m.c.
and thousands of people turn out   and clayton
eshleman and i   being among the main poet organizers wind
up the delegated peacekeepers sitting by the stage looking
out for trouble   while shirley clarke who is setting up to
film the proceedings is talking with the village voice

25

reporter and paul blackburn is giving an interview in french
to two guys with a nagra and the place is gradually filling
up when piero heliczer comes by

he's a poet who's been out of
town he's just gotten back and wants to read   but clayton
who's gotten stuck with the job of making up a schedule tells
him the program is already too long and theres just no room
    then we get the bad news   marlene had to go to london
and we have to make do with ed sanders and the fugs   which
may have been all right because they were celebrities to
most people   but they were just some more poets to us

        finally the readings begin   and theyre kind of
weird   the crowd is so big that when it claps or laughs
    it claps and laughs very slow   its some kind of giant
good natured retard   like lenny out of *of mice and men*
    when its my turn to read   i used to read in those days
    and everybody gets a chance to read about two poems
    i started to read one poem about how we must help our
friends in vietnam   only i wasnt sure who my friends were
    in vietnam or whether i had any   and i thought it was a
mildly funny poem   but the laughter from the audience
    started up like a storm   a slow storm   because it took
them about thirty seconds after a line was over to start
    laughing at it   and i was a bit unnerved the lines were
at a human talking speed and i couldnt really slow them down
    too much because i would sound like a comedian milking his
jokes   but i had to do something or the storm would break
    in the middle of a new line burying it along with the next
one   and once they started laughing it was like i was
moving through a sea of molasses   swimming through this
thick liquid   trying to retime my sense of the waves
    because they were laughing in slow motion and they
could be a line and a half back   and they didnt get
everything anyway   so i could never be sure exactly what
they were laughing at

but i get through it and do an icy
formal litany filled with darkness death and destruction and
i feel better   because they keep silent till about half a
minute after im done   when they finally realize its over

26

and they start to applaud   and im even more bewildered
when a giant in a big overcoat leaps onto the stage to
   embrace me
                 "if you give me copy   i will translate and
   print poem in pravda"   and im so confused i give him my
book and go sit down on the edge of the stage until just
before the intermission when the fugs go on with a musical
   number   then we're all standing around for a while
backstage laughing at the grubby condition of the backstage
of this second avenue rock palace thats so run down they dont
even fix the ceiling leaks they just leave out a rain pail
   which they never bother to empty and it stinks
                                           and we're
interrupted by some commotion out front where a speed freak
is stealing shirley clarke's camera   and we chase after him
up the aisle and out into the street   where shirley finally
   tackles him and makes him give it back   by the time we
return to the theater people are filing back in and the fugs
are playing again till the poets have time to get back on
   the stage   where im sitting with john ashbery and several
other poets all waiting to go on

            john is very patient   he's something of a hero
worshipper and he's really anxious to hear voznesensky read
      john's met him briefly uptown at a party the other day
and he confesses that he almost asked for an autograph
      meanwhile theres a bottle of brandy under the table
we're sitting at and some of the poets who havent read yet
   have been discreetly taking sips from it   and john hasnt
read yet and he's really nervous because of the size of the
crowd   so he's pretty much taken possession of the bottle
   and whenever he thinks nobody is looking he takes another
shot from it   pretty soon he's hardly nervous at all and
leaning back in his chair happily or leaning forward and
   scowling in mock concentration or tipping back to sneak
another shot from the bottle   and finally its voznesenskys
turn to read
              john is all attention because voznesensky makes
a little speech in cautious english   somebody reads one of
his poems in english and it doesnt sound any better than i

thought it would   then voznesensky reads it in russian
and this is something none of us is prepared for   he has
two registers   one forte fortissimo which sounds like
marshal timoshenko haranguing his troops   and the other
pian pianissimo in the voice of a lover breathing *ya ti
liublyoo* into the ear of his mistress   and he moves between
the two registers with the clocklike regularity of a russian
pop singer at "the twin guitars"   john giggles and the
audience goes wild

voznesensky reads a few poems like this and john is
getting very giggly and is reaching back for another drink
when voznesensky goes up to the microphone and once again
in english tells everyone   "i am going to read one poem in
russian with no translation   because russian is simple
language what sounds just like means   this poem called
bells"

john is all attention   he has the bottle half way to
his lips and stops   and voznesensky launches into this
flood of russian tintinnabulation in which nearly every
word sounds like ding or dong   john gets hysterical the
chair tips over backwards and goes all the way down to the floor
where he quietly passes out

while the crowd roars for
voznesensky i rescue whats left of the bottle and with the
help of my neighbor quietly lift john back to the table and
go off to sit in the audience for the rest of the reading
which ends with jackson mac low holding an american flag
and reading a good but nearly endless poem that goes on so
long that people are leaving in droves   and piero heliczer
runs backstage and comes front carrying the rain pail while
jackson imperviously continues to read and i start to run
toward the stage with the bottle still in my hand   but i
get there too late because piero has emptied the contents of
the bucket into the audience spilling its liquid all over
shirley clarke's camera and the village voice reporter

the soaking reporter interviews a bunch of the poets
to find out what was going on and nobody is really sure
but ed sanders explains it to her   it was just a rain
pail   but with all those poets standing around back there

waiting to go on guzzling up beer and with no john back
there
     "it was a pail of piss" he said smiling at her gently
out of his baby blue eyes   "guggenheim poets piss"

     the next day i read a long account of the three-penny
poets reading for peace in the village voice that featured
     "an impassioned performance by the russian poet andrei
voznesensky" that "came to a bizarre ending during a reading
by jackson mac low when the poet piero heliczer for mysterious
     reasons rushed up on stage and drenched the audience with a
pail of urine"

i ran into austin gallagher on the way to the bookstore
and he told me some friends were putting together a reading
in the grove celebrating spring and love   and i guess i
looked a little doubtful because doug rothschild called me
a few days later to remind me that we were going to have a
reading on the themes of love and noise   but when i got
there i found out that jean luc namcy had heard that we were
celebrating love and laws and gave a reading from plato
and doug told me he had said "love and loss"   so i
thought i had been right in the first place and i would talk
about

spring love
noise and all

          but i wondered what i would talk about   because
here in southern california youre never really sure when
spring begins   i mean the experience of spring   the
vernal equinox is one thing   but spring is something else
     and ive been living out here twenty years and i cant
always tell when its spring
                              my guess is it comes on some time
in late february   and you hardly notice it   a few branch
ends turn yellow a few wildflowers begin to sprout an
occasionally different bird appears   and you figure it
might as well be spring

          now thats a little different from springs i
remember where i came from   in the east when its spring
     boy are you ready for it   if you lived in new york
city or upstate new york about 130 miles north of the city
     the way you'd know spring was coming was that around the
end of march you'd hear rolls of thunder or cannonades that
     would mean the ice was breaking on the river you'd say gee
it must be spring the ice is breaking on the river   and it
was like a series of deep distant drum rolls
brrrrrrrrrrmbrrrrrrrrrrrm   and you didn't feel much
better about it   because the sky was still gray and cold
and the trees were still bare

          in fact you felt better in january because the snow
seemed to keep you warm especially when the temperature got
down around zero and the snow was piled up around the house
and along the roadside   because after every snow the snow
     ploughs would clear out the road and pile up the snow along
the roadside into a wall from six to ten feet high that

31

would shield the houses from the wind and you'd shovel out a
pathway to the street   but inside it was warm   and pretty
  much everybody in this little town of north branch felt
insulated and warm and pretty good in january as long as the
  heating fuel held out   and they didnt feel too bad in
february either

             but when the spring came   in march   and you
heard the dull cannonade on the river   thats when you
started to feel bad   because it had been so cold and bare
and gray   and you had been holding out so long for the
wild mustard and the goldfinches   and maybe the coming of
the quince   that the sound coming off the river   that
  seemed to promise an entry into the land of the hearts
desire   which you knew would take another month at least
  made you feel real bad

             so thats why when the spring came to north branch at
the end of march   it seemed that every year two people would
hang themselves off their back porch   because they couldnt
  wait anymore

             but there was the other side of spring and you
expected great things of it   because you had read all those
  marvelous sweet and jingling poems by those provençal
bullshitters waiting for spring to come so they could go out
  into the fields and fuck and kill people   brash and noisy
poems that went on as i remenber something like "oh spring is
here the birds are singing lets go out and fight some
  battles and make it in the grass" in a cheerful jingling and
very overrated way
                           that my friend paul blackburn did the best
he could with   which was to bury the jingle and jazz up the
noise a bit   to make them sound a little bit like ezra
pound and a little bit like paul doing an east village macho
  number   and a lot better than they sound to my ears in
provençal   and with poetic generosity he covered up the
banality of their vocabulary and their tedious ideas if you
  could call their attitudes ideas and it all sounded so
cheerful that we thought it must have been a good idea to sit
  in toulouse and welcome in the spring

  32

but dont you believe it   toulouse is a dreadful
place and nobody wants to be there   everyone in toulouse
would rather be in paris   so if you have a choice about
the spring you dont want to spend it in toulouse

                                        paul actually
lived there for a while   and he was always running off to
paris or mallorca or to spain

          but wherever you are you are likely to have this
idea of what it means for spring to come   and you know how
it will come and when it will come   because in your
expectations it always comes   in a neat order the way
   seasons do   because there are exactly four of them and
they are very nicely named and there are exactly three months
in them and they very obediently follow the astronomical year

          i once figured out a system for the southern
california year   i dont know if anyone understands it
   but i once sat down and figured it out   nothing about
this climate seemed to follow the pattern of my orderly
astronomical year   not its weather its seasons or even the
variations within a single california day

                                   so i sat down and
   worked it out   at least to my own satisfaction for the
stretch of coast extending from tijuana to santa barbara i
   dont know anything about monterey or oakland or san
francisco   but i think i understand the coast of
   southern california at least from santa barbara to the
mexican border

                    the key to it is the afternoon a warm and
luminous sunlit afternoon   all year long there is some
   point in the day   however short   maybe only an hour that
is filled with warm sunlight

                              in the middle of december this
   might be only an hour somewhere between two and three and
maybe its a little pallid and not quite so warm as the
beginning of a sunlit morning some time in summer   but its
there   even at the winter solstice   if nothing else
intervenes   like a little fog or rain   but thats an
intervention i'll talk about later because in principle the
sun is always there even in the dead of winter

now as the days get longer this point of sunlight
expands   gets brighter warmer and lasts longer   and what
we have is an expanding afternoon   that lasts at first one
hour then an hour and a half and maybe two   until by what
we call summer   its expanded to engulf almost the entire
day   and then it starts to contract again growing slowly
  and progressively shorter and cooler through the autumnal
equinox   shrinking to the same bright point at the winter
solstice   from which it starts again   and because there
are three dimensions to this afternoon   brightness heat and
temporal duration   i think of this sunlit substance i'm
  calling afternoon as a kind of solid

                                        which because it
expands and contracts continuously and simultaneously along
all three dimensions   i see as a kind of luminous warm cone
    or more precisely as an unending series of connected
cones lying flat along the continuum of time   a kind of
brancusi "endless column" lying down

              now it doesnt really feel like this or not
completely   there are periodic and minor interruptions
    like rain or cloudy skies that temporarily obscure the
pure periodic perfection of this expanding and contracting
luminous cone   and theyre bunched in clusters

                                        the rain
  almost all of it comes in what we conventionally call
november and december or sometimes january or february
    but the key to grasping this is to realize that it all
comes bunched in two or three day clusters that disappear and
reveal the ongoing and constantly growing or shrinking sunlit
afternoon   there is also the overcast of june or sometimes
may   a thick cloud cover that for a long time continues to
obscure the true climate   but this too i see as merely a
  longer interruption   to understand this all you have to
do is get on a plane and climb a few hundred feet to see that
the serious business of the sunlight has never been
  interrupted

              now there are a few other facts ive negelected
to mention   the santa anna   a sirocco-like wind blowing
off the mountains toward the water that establishes a hotter

drier moment for a week or even two   this can occur almost
any time of the year but seems most often in winter   now
 this intervention makes any section of the cone seem hotter
  longer and brighter   but this is also an illusion that is
 merely a coupling effect that by burning off the cloud cover
earlier and keeping it off longer simply reveals the full
 extent and heat of whatever segment of the sunlit cone is
then present

              so you see the weather of california is a
    simple and even monotonous business   beautiful as it is
     but monotonous as all beautiful things must be   an
unendingly ongoing expanding and contracting cone of sunlight
    randomly or maybe not so randomly   but arbitrarily
 intersected by brief invasions of rain or cloud or santa
annas   and there are no seasons at all only expansions and
 contractions of an afternoon that generate this continuously
 shrinking and expanding cone of light and heat in which
theres nothing to wait for but the brief invasions of the
 rain and fog and desert wind

              but in new york you really had something to wait
  for   you knew you had three months coming that would be
pretty much the same   and then things would change   maybe
 for the better   and thats why you waited for spring
   · because things were going to be neat   youd have a neat
 spring   and neat is the right word for it because its very
   much like the ideas surrounding the spring
                                    we had a quince
tree once   it was actually a quince tree outside a house
 that we were renting from a local dairy farmer   and when
  the spring came it began to blossom with beautiful red
 flowers   so that you thought of the spring as holding out
a promise of these bright red flowers   but in all those
  springs i only saw it flower once   because with spring
  the buds began to open and a sudden frost would come that
  killed all the flowers   and as long as i was up there we
never did get any quince
                        which was a little like the black and
  brown striped caterpillars that also came out in spring
       but i remember a sunny warm october an indian summer

that some of these little jerks came out thinking it was
spring   crawling around and probably expecting in their
infinite innocence to be turned into colorful butterflies
    and were turned by the cold into furry little black and
brown caterpillar corpses instead
                            and there was a certain
murderousness in this   as this second spring came out to
clobber all those little bastards before they got a chance to
fuck   as my friend ted berrigan might have said

            because that seemed to matter a lot to ted
    although maybe no more than the pills or pepsi that
finally took ted away so much too soon   though i dont know
whether it was spring or not   but it felt awfully grim when
i heard he'd gone away and ted was cheerful enough to be his
own spring but even he couldnt hold up against the weather

            so thinking about the arrangement of spring
    and its perfect organization   and then thinking of what
spring means as an original heating up of the system   and
of how as a system heats up it gets noisier and things start
    to buzz around less controllably and bump into other things
    and how some of these collisions may be joyful and some
of them seem like theyre going to be more joyful than they
turn out to be
                    i thought about one spring when i was looking
forward to good things   i was living in greenwich village
on a one block street in one of those comfortable little
apartments that was so cheap i could pay the rent with half
a day's work   it was old and small   and it was on the
fifth floor of a walkup that was built so long ago it had
slave quarters in the back   and i had to share a bathroom
with my neighbor across the floor   but it had three rooms
gas heat and a fireplace   and i could see the hudson and
the palisades from my living room window i could smell fresh
bread from the italian bakery across the street and it only
cost me eighteen dollars and seventy-five cents a month
    which included a rent raise of 15% over the last tenant
    and the woman i shared the bathroom with was someone i
was having an intricate relationship with

36

she was a very attractive blond soprano a
coloratura who was struggling with her upper register
which wasnt light or bright enough because her middle
and lower registers were dark and lustrous and maybe she
wasnt a true coloratura after all but her voice teacher swore
she was   and she was struggling with this and also i think
with being a mormon a jack mormon or lapsed mormon   who
didnt go to church and wasn't living the kind of life she was
supposed to live   and i suppose she was struggling with
this   and there was our relationship   which was at
intervals passionate and stormy and probably not doing her a
lot of good with all her other troubles   but it was the
springtime when people come out of their apartments and begin
to hang around the park where the trees are flowering and
the old guys are playing checkers and bocci

and it was the kind of particularly mild
spring that comes to new york once every four or five years
the kind i remembered as a kid with sunny showers drying
warmly on your shirt and carrying maple flowers in small
rivulets down the curb   and this year it brought out a
crop of homeless people
the reagan government didnt invent
homelessness they merely perfected it
but these were mostly
kids who'd left parental jails in ohio or indiana to look for
real life on the streets of the big city and this spring
they were camping out
a number of them had found out there
were a lot of flat roofs in the village and a lot of people
who didnt care if they slept up there   as long as they
didnt hold too many parties or make too much noise   so they
would stash their bedrolls up at the top of the stairs above
the top floor of one of the walkups a few buildings down
from where they slept   to be less conspicuous and keep
them out of the rain   i lived on the top floor and i'd
noticed these two guys and a girl who i supposed were living
on a rooftop somewhere down the block   and one sunday
morning i was going down to get the times and pick up some
fresh baked bread and cheese because this was the week that

37

according to ugo her teacher ruth had found her upper
register   and we were going to have a celebratory breakfast

                    and i was halfway down the block across from cino's
and not far from the bleecker street boys club   when i was
stopped by a crowd of people gathered around two cop cars
that had parked in the middle of the road   one of the cops
had the blankets and bedrolls and was on the radio   and in
the back of the car was the girl a skinny teenager in jeans
and military jacket with a pretty face blotched from crying
      i figured someone had finally blown the whistle on our
roof dwellers   last night's party must have been too loud
      and the cops were busting them while all my italian
neighbors were standing around talking looking and pointing
at the girl and up into a building on my side of the street
out of which two other cops pushed one of the two boys
      a sullen dark haired kid with pock marks into the back
of the other car
                        the conversation was in sicilian but the
gist of it now came clear   a very old sicilian lady looking up
at the roof explained it to the woman from zampieri's bakery
      "he wanted to marry her and she refused him and he was
going to jump off the roof"
                              meditating on this excess of
passion i wandered off to the park instead of the cheese
store where i ran into a friend of mine i hadn't seen in over
a year   we got to talking and into a chess game that was
eccentric and complicated and lasted almost an hour   so
that when i got home ruth was angry and suspicious i told her
about the police bust and the imaginary suicide threat and
about running into gene and the game of chess   but she
didnt seem to understand   she said she didnt believe me
that i was making it all up and that i'd slipped out to go
fucking somebody else   and she began screaming and throwing
things and almost hit her cat rasputin who ran under the
couch to hide   and i apologized for a while till i got
tired of it and got mad and started yelling back till i got
tired of that and all the noise and screaming and breaking
things and went back to my apartment across the hall where
i sat looking out at the flowering sycamore in front of the

38

bakery smoldering and reflecting on the uncertainties of
spring till i heard a knock at the door and figured it was
    time to go make up   but it wasn't ruth

                outside the door was another friend   and she
had a bottle of champagne in one hand and a jar of caviar in
the other   she looked up at me with laughing eyes held up
    the caviar and pointed toward the couch

                "its spring   i thought we might celebrate"
and i took a good look at my friend her beautiful sexy little body
her great lovely eyes her funny freckles on one side of her
    nose and her slightly overfull mouth to make sure that i
wasn't dreaming just because it was spring

                and as we sat on my couch and talked i thought
    about how nice this would all be and how simple and i
thought of my serious quarrel and my complicated relationship
with my hysterical friend across the hall   i put my friends
    caviar back in the bag put the champagne bottle back in her
hand kissed her on the nose pushed her gently out the door
and explained we would have to take this up some time later
        and i did the serious thing i went back to my quarrel
and my complicated relation with my hysterical friend
        which i believe ended three weeks later

        so much for spring

in april of 1981 i was invited to a conference on
the avant-garde that was to be held in iowa city and i was
a little surprised   for all i knew iowa was a state of
complacent farmers who raised hogs and corn and had a
university whose art and writing programs generated equally
bland products   at the same time most of the art world
seemed to be returning to somewhat less bland but equally
predictable painted products   so it seemed like a strange
time and place for a conference on the avant-garde   it was
news to me that the university of iowa housed an extensive
dada archive and under the shelter of some odd department
or other   also harbored a group of experimental video
artists and tolerated   a loosely connected artist
performance group   so the art historians who managed the
dada archive invited a number of other art historians and
critics   roz krauss ed fry and a few others   to talk
about the early 20th century avant-garde   along with the
three richards   kostelanetz schechner and higgins and
jerry rothenberg and me   to give some kind of reading
of the contemporary situation

when i got to the campus a tornado was threatening
thunder and lightning were storming outside while
richard kostelanetz was defining the avant-garde from the
stage of a crowded hall   but the tornado missed us   the
next day was sunny   little ducks were walking around the
campus and richard schechner was lamenting a decline from
the traditions of the heroic avant-garde sixties and
prophesying our entry into a terrible and dull new time

what it means
to be avant-garde

because i knew there was going to be a kind of
transition between the readings that i knew we were going to
have here and the kind of talking i do   i thought i would
surprise everybody by   bringing a couple of clippings from
newspapers and reading from them along with my talking   and
i decided this improvisatorily   in the manner of my
talking   as i came upon them   fortuitously   on the
plane coming from san diego
                                i'm something of a newspaper buff
and setting off this day in an airplane heading east
toward iowa city   over denver   with a copy of the san
diego union   something made me want to read this copley
newspaper   which like many local newspapers   once you
get past the first few pages   is filled with stories of
surprising and unlikely things   to which i have an
attraction   as i have an attraction to a newspapers
organization   an attraction shared by many artists
possibly because of its fractured collage-like structure
and as we flew out over the rising mountains immediately
to the east of san diego i was struck by the title of a one
column story

COLOR THE ISLES SOFT PINK

christo   the story continued   the artist who gave
the world the VALLEY CURTAIN in the colorado rockies and
the RUNNING FENCE in california   now wants to color the
islands of biscayne bay pink   the controversial artist
unveiled his newest project tuesday
                               how curious this language
sounds when you read it out loud

41

                                          he plans to cover ten
uninhabited islands in the bay which separates miami from
  miami beach with   silky soft   pink   polypropylene
fabric   because the islands are not entirely uninhabited
    if one considers all the world's inhabitants   something
more gets said   the effect the artist said   would be of a
  series of glowing water lilies   an homage to claude monets
    water lily paintings
                                  like any artist   christo said   i
will have my water lilies
                                  he said the project would be
  entitled

SURROUNDED ISLANDS PROJECT FOR BISCAYNE BAY
GREATER MIAMI

      it would cost from eight hundred thousand to one million
dollars   and the money would come from the sale of the
  drawings and collages of the project   so its an ecological
project   of a sort   except for the polypropylene   the
  work was commissioned by the
            NEW WORLD FESTIVAL OF THE ARTS
and planned for june 4 to june 26 1982 in miami   the
  festival also features new plays by arthur miller edward
albee and tennessee williams
                                  theres something about reading
newspapers thats like throwing the i ching

        now christo also said   and this is what i was
coming to   that he had consulted with environmentalists and
  government agencies on this project and he had run into no
objections   though he had not yet secured the required
  permits
                  our new department of the interior must have proved
fairly easy

        according to christo helicopters would drop the
fabric onto the islands over a ten mile stretch of bay from
downtown miami to sunny isles   then a crew of four hundred
  would pull the pink cocoon into place all at once   and his
water lilies would then remain in place for two weeks before
  coming down
                          it would be enchanting   not imposing or menacing

  42

but intimate and lyrical the artist promised
                                        this sounds like
my old collage poetry again   but i want to consider this
from the point of view of questions concerning the avant-
garde
           now im not proposing christo as an avant-garde artist
           but if this art is avant-garde its not very challenging
           to the chamber of commerce of greater miami   because
the chamber of commerce is perfectly cheerful about it   and
somebody is running interference for it with the rest of the
people of miami   probably lots of people   though mainly
jeanne claude   and the work will get done   i have no
doubt   and i have no doubt that it will be juxtaposed with
other avant-garde works by arthur miller tennessee williams
and edward albee

           about the same time or shortly after i came upon
another article that raised similar questions for me   it
was one of those days when i was absolutely starved for news
and wherever i looked i found it   and this article read

ACTOR KEEPS HIS HEAD BUT KILLER DOESNT

     every actor wants to be a movie star says joe spinell
and everybody else wants to be in the movies including the
usherettes
                this is in a section called THE ARTS   spinell is
a new york born character actor who decided that one way to
become a star was to write and produce your own film
     which he did and he put himself in the lead   the film
he wrote is called MANIAC and is about a psychotic killer
who murders and mutilates beautiful women
                                        spinell gives a
learned account of the plot structure   its based on modern
day killers who had problems with their mothers   the style
     here he turns to film history   through the killers
eyes   is taken from the peter lorre movie M
                                        well maybe
lorre is not the auteur   but thats all right we're close
     but unlike the lorre classic   according to the writer
in the san diego union   MANIAC has such an abundance of

43

blood that it is difficult to get distributed by home box
   office or any of the other regular distributors   in fact
   the los angeles times in a sudden access of morality has
   refused to take ads for the film because the victim gets his
   revenge on the maniac by tearing his head off full camera

              why did spinell use so much violence?   to compete
   says the forty year old actor   we had to come up with
   something new
                     now is joe spinell in the avant-garde   making
   it new?   its maybe not clear   because joe spinell will tell
   you   "look dont tell me about violence and blood because
   then i have to talk about ABC and CBS   for twenty-two years
   theyve been bringing us the vietnamese war"
                                          political morality
   enters here   this is a moral form of the avant-garde   but
   he takes this no further   just says im making movies for
   people to enjoy   "if you want art go to a museum   people
   give me money to make a movie to make money   thats why
   we're called an industry the movie industry   the industry
   is in trouble and television is partly to blame   people are
   inundated by tv and their brains are numb"
                                       moralizing
   educational and avant-garde roles are all preempted by
   movie maker joe spinell   there appears to be no place to go
   here between lyrical intimate commercial avant-garde artist
   christo and avant-garde didactic moralist commercial shocker
   joe spinell

           and i was thinking about this while i was flying
   toward iowa and thinking about how everyone was going to be
   trying to locate the avant-garde   and about how almost
   everyone was going to agree that it would involve either
   shocking or making it new   and that i was supposed to be
   talking about this too   and i realized i was going to be
   confused   because practically every role classically
   attributed to the avant-garde has been preempted by something
   else   and i reflected that i myself have never really had
   a clear image of what it was to be avant-garde   though ive
   been thrust into the role often enough to know what it feels
   like to be avant-garde

   44

a friend of mine had written a book
marjorie perloff had written a book dealing with american
poetry as a kind of french connection   as opposed to the
english connection which is conventionally supposed for it
in the schools   now i personally think there are many
roots to contemporary american poetry   certainly my poetry
and the poetry i admire   but i also know what writing a
book means   in a book you have to organize your ideas
pretty much one thing at a time   if its an important thing
and you want to really get it done   and this is a book
designed to challenge what i have always thought of as the
anglophiliac model of american poetry that is so dominant in
those literary strongholds east of the mississippi   or the
connecticut river   north of the monongahela   that are so
strongly devoted to an anglican passion   that they give
the impression of some kind of outpost in a novel by huxley
or evelyn waugh   where the people are sitting around on a
veranda sipping their gin slings in the shade of the local
textile factory or integrated circuit fabricating plant
dreaming of playing polo or cricket or rugby in the greener
older playing fields at eton or harrow   which they may
never have seen   being often second generation eastern
european jews from brooklyn or queens   or lithuanians from
indiana or lutherans from wisconsin   and somehow there
they are gathered on the veranda in new haven or manhattan
in memory of the british empire   of which they are among
the last supports   and several columns of which this book
is probably intended to take away

                                  or maybe more precisely
this book is only bringing the news to these outposts
that the british empire has long since passed away   and
that the messages from england would no longer be coming and
had not been coming for a long time   and that there was a
french connection as there is a russian connection and a
spanish connection   and for many a chinese connection or
japanese connection   there are lots of connections in this
world   but in a book you have to do one thing at a time
the world may not happen one thing at a time but in a book
you have to tell one thing at a time
                            and my friend was invited

45

to washington to be part of a discourse with some of these
english emigres and refugees   among whom were numbered
    harold bloom and john hollander and richard howard   who
are certainly distinguished members of the refugee community

                    now marjorie was giving a talk based on the
last chapter of her most recent book   *the poetics of
indeterminacy*   the last chapter of which happens to deal
with john cage and with me

                              and whatever differences there may
be between cage and me   and these are considerable   we
were both obliterated by the righteous wrath of harold bloom
    who had hardly heard more than our names   when he
denounced the proceedings as ridiculous and us as nonpoets
and stormed off the stage

                              i was told about this performance of
blooms and thought it was wonderful and forgot about it
    but it was not long afterward that i was invited out to
the very same place to do a talk performance on the folger
librarys little shakespearean stage   and it happened that
when i came to do the performance i had something serious in
    mind   because a friend of mine had died two or three days
before   after a sudden and unexpected hospitalization from
which we had all hoped she would come out alive   and i
wanted to make my piece a kind of homage   a meditation and
speculation on the nature of her life and death

                    so in the course of things i told her story
    or what i knew of it   and i tried to consider the
nature of the fit   between the life we lead and the death
we get   and what i wanted to think about was whether there
was such a fit and if there was   what kind it was   and i
did the best i could   under the circumstances   of being
there   then   which is my image of what an artist does and
is   somebody who does the best he can   under the
circumstances   without worrying about making it new or
shocking   because the best you can do depends upon what you
have to do and where   and if you have to invent something
new to do the work at hand you will   but not if you have a
ready-made that will work and is close at hand and you want
to get on with the rest of the business

46

then youll pick up
the tool thats there   a tool that somebody else has made
    that will work   and youll lean on it and feel grateful
when its good to you   for somebody elses work   and youll
think of him as a friend who would borrow as freely from you
if he thought of it or needed to   because there is a
community of artists   who dont recognize copyrights and
patents   or shouldnt   except under unusual circumstances
        who send each other tools in the mail or exchange them
in conversation in a bar
                        though i had a couple of friends
from whom i got a lot of things in the mail   who got very
nervous about exchanging things with each other because they
had ileana sonnabend looking over their shoulders   and one
of them got so distressed because he had ileana looking over
his shoulder forbidding him to collaborate with the other
    friend   that when he wrote the text for the others
installation performance he never put his name on it   but
this is an unusual situation   and i only mention it because
of that

                    and i was there in washington doing the best i
could   borrowing when i could and inventing when i had to
    and the audience was tolerant and reasonable   and
listened to me doing the best i could   and when i was
through there was a small gathering of people who came up to
talk with me   because when you talk to people they
naturally want to talk to you   because theyve had some of
you presented to them   and a discourse has been initiated
    or suggested   at least in my kind of poetry   which is
intended to open a discourse and not close it   a discourse
that can go on with or without me once ive contributed to it
        and the first question that anybody asked me as we were
standing around the punch bowl was what do you think of
harold bloom?
                    i said im sorry   i dont think of harold
bloom   they said but could you think of harold bloom?   i
said i could think of harold bloom   i could think of harold
bloom if i wanted to   you want me to? all right   i'll
try   they said what does harold bloom have against you?   i

47

said   its not personal   they said   but he seemed so
   angry   he thinks i'm trying to kill him   its an emigre
condition i said   you imagine people are threatening you
   from outside   and everything outside seems terribly
threatening   i dont blame him for being angry   if i
thought somebody was trying to kill me i might be angry at
them   im not trying to kill harold bloom
                                        they said   then
really why was he so angry?

                              well i said i think hes
suffering from a case of mistaken identity
                                        they said whats
that?
     i said   first he thinks hes part of a great tradition
   he's not   second he thinks hes a critic of poetry he's
not   and then he thinks he knows what the world of poetry
consists of   but he doesnt
                         they said what do you mean by
that?   and i said look   years ago   the first time i
ever heard of harold bloom   he came to my attention by
accident   somebody i knew   an editor for an east coast
publishing house   who now works for the national endowment
   said to me   you have to read this its extraordinary   it
was a work on william blake   it was not extraordinary   it
was what you would expect from an academic literary critic
   with a taste for romanticism   a more or less plausible
account of blake as a complex and ironic poet that might have
pleased any new critic   except that blake wasnt a catholic
or anglican or even a presbyterian   but some kind of funny
   homemade   secular   religionist   whose gospel tended
to make most of the new critics laugh   both because it was
funny and because they had a strong taste for institutional
   orthodoxy
                    but from harold bloom you dont get a sense that
theres anything funny about casting allegorical epics with a
set of entities that have names like orc and urthona and
oothoon in places or states with names like golgonooza or
   ulro   which blake comments on through a set of quirky
drawings that make him one of the first and most peculiar
concrete poets to work in english

   48

but from harold bloom you dont get any sense at
all only an explanation   so i didnt think he was
extraordinary at all but rather ordinary   and like most
academic critics rather useless   until he extended himself
  beyond romantic poetry   or appeared to   and offered
what he called a theory of poetry

                              now its not really a theory
    because its not at all testable and has no explanatory
  power   it is in fact only a suggestion described as a
theory   about the way poets who are not yet poets   come
  to be poets through the poetry of the poets   that have preceded
them   which as a suggestion is not in itself extraordinary
    but in the way bloom works this out   which is fairly
extraordinary   as a struggle of sons with the ghosts of
  their poetical fathers   from whom they have learned what
  they want their poetry to be   and whose poetical powers
they want to acquire and consider their own

                              now what is
  extraordinary is not blooms seedy freudianism   the oedipal
struggle between fathers and sons   which has continued to
be fashionable in academic literary circles far longer than
  its nineteenth-century imagery would suggest   but the
object of the struggle   a poetical style or perhaps a
poetical content   in any case a poetical product   that
  bloom sees as a kind of commodity over which there is a
  copyright dispute

                              this is quite extraordinary and very funny
    especially since as far as bloom is concerned there are
very few of these poetical products and they appear to have
been disputed for centuries   since each father had a father
with whom he must in turn have disputed the rights   so
poor john ashbery must have wallace stevens for a father
    who   you may not believe this   will have whitman
for his father who will have emerson as his   as emily
  dickinson will also   and pound may have browning who
will have shelley who will have wordsworth who will have
  milton who will have spenser who will found the line   the
abraham of post-enlightenment poetry

                              but what is this product
  and what use could it possibly be in any time if it remained

the same over all that time   three drastically different
centuries

        but for bloom time and culture count for nearly
nothing   cabalists and calvinists english lords   brooklyn
journalists hartford insurance executives and new york art
critics   as poets confront nothing but death and the crises
of the personal ego   so the whole line of blooms contending
"strong poets" turns out to be only the textbook version of
english romanticism   suitably trivialized and egotized by
bloom and called the tradition

        now i have very little
interest in what anybody would call a tradition and no
interest in anything you could call a canon   but i can see
the service bloom has rendered graduate students of english
literature   he has reduced for them the great number of
poets to a handful of "strong" ones   who turn out to be
the most familiar ones of the textbooks   and set his
students to work finding their poet fathers   for which
task he has equipped them with a mongrel array of greek and
hebrew technical terms   useful i suppose mainly to console
them for their lack of ability to read in any other language
than english

        while for the rest of the general educated
public   if they read him   he has created the consolatory
sense of the increasing belatedness and progressively more
attenuated virtues of each successive generation of poets
from blake and wordsworth to the present   encouraging this
reader or nonreader to take comfort from his ignorance of the
dozens of contemporary poets working in his language   that
it would most probably not have been worth his trouble to
make their acquaintance at all

        and thats what i told this man
in washington   or something to that effect   and what i
realized as i said it then   and realize as i say it now
    there is something of an idea of the avant-garde in
harold bloom   however inverted   and even he seems more at
home with it than i am   a notion of first comers whose
achievements were new and blocked the way to further
achievements along the same path   an idea of patented
inventions   each one acting as a roadblock   and the

tradition as a series of bitterly fought retreats till the last
"strong" poet finds himself like kafkas rodent or a beckett
character backed into the last corner of the room   its a
funny view of a tradition   having it back you into a corner
and comically a little like clement greenbergs version
of modernist painting   in which the brilliant achievement
of one artist closes an avenue to the next   but actually
rather more like the architecture of florence   where genius
has choked up the traffic and wont let you renovate the
streets

but at least the tradition of art history is
based on a serious cultural ideology   on the preeminence
and power of the nineteenth-century industrial state that
traced the marvel of its own spiritual development in a
history that began with an ingenious geography

for as michel
de certeau has pointed out in his great book on "the writing
of history"   all history begins with geography   first you
mark out the place where it all happened   and this
demarcation of the historical place creates along its
boundaries the nonhistorical place   where nothing has
happened in any developmental way   and there is no history
only anthropology   because there are only the customs
and traditions and rituals that maintain   the primitive
traditional?   self   because history is the allegorical
epic of the development of the civilized citizen self

so art history has been worked out as a
fantastical progress   from the fertile crescent to egypt
in a few skips across the mediterranean to greece
over the adriatic to italy   across the alps to
culminate in paris   or perhaps london or berlin   from ur
to the eiffel tower   or if you choose literature   from
nimrod to arnold bennett or thomas mann   which in the
interests of a purely illusory sanity is foreshortened in
the schools and taught as the tradition of painting from
giotto to picasso which is no less maniacal   only less
intelligible   because it reduces hegels outrageous but
understandable pilgrimage from slavery to the freedom of the
german state to an intellectual rubble or pile of bric-a-brac

which is a junk heap not a tradition   and to which the
only adequate response may be nietzsches comment that german
    culture and education   for this read european
institutionalized culture is no culture at all   only
a deeply entrenched barbarism   but of course in the united
  states institutionalized culture is not a deeply entrenched
barbarism   it is only a sickly barbarism   barely clinging
 to the saddle
                        so when it speaks   or groans   which is
perhaps more appropriate for harold bloom   of its tradition
    it is not speaking from any particular institutional
  authority   just a provincial place in new haven
                                            which is
why i do not normally think of harold bloom and his tradition
  except as an entertainment and as somebody asks me in the
  present   because all that unites us in this country is
 the present   and the difficulty of recognizing it and
 occupying it   which is why its so easy to slip into
prophesy and the emptiness of the future   that is so easy
  to occupy because of its emptiness   that we fill up so
 quickly with a cargo of memories and attendant dreams

                        so just a moment ago richard schechner was
trying to tell us about the present state of the avant-garde
    and gave us a cautionary account of how everything in
  theater and performance now was a decline from the
revolutionary great old days   how even the best of the new
artists are merely indulging in degraded versions of the
  great techniques of the revolutionary predecessors instead
 of carrying on and developing the tradition   while even
the best of the old are no longer capable of going on in
 their avant-garde way   but are at best repeating
themselves   and then he cautioned us that the loss of this
  tradition of the sixties would cost us dearly   as the new
   fascism of the reagan government was almost upon us and we
 would once again need revolutionary artists to lead a new
resistance

                        and i marveled to hear this nostalgic account
 of the great past   and cautionary account of the terrible
future accompanying so trivial a grip on the present   in

52

the mouth of an avowed member of what for the lack of a
better term we could call the sixties avant-garde   but
maybe thats the problem with the notion of the avant-garde
that it turns itself from a discourse into a tradition
whose members worry about its decline in a threatening
future   and maybe thats why i'm such a poor avant-gardist
because i'm mainly concerned with the present   which
if i can find it might let me know what to do   and as for
the future   it will find us all by itself   whether we look
backwards or forwards it will be there at the top of the
stairs   meanwhile i want to occupy the present

and what is it at this moment in the united states
a rocketing inflation that no particular politician can
make anything other than a rash claim to understand   a
rising unemployment that anyone can understand and
underestimate as they understand   because as the number of
people who lose their employment increases   so the number
of people who are no longer eligible for unemployment
compensation who become demoralized and no longer appear at
the unemployment offices looking for employment or the help
they can no longer receive   increases as well   and these
people disappear from the numbers of the unemployed as they
cease to be counted among the job hunting poor   who as they
are no longer counted dont count and become some kind of
indefinitely numerous ghosts   who no longer live in our
affluent or struggling economy   but trouble it mysteriously
nonetheless
and if for a long time i didnt know what it
meant to be haunted i begin to know it now   in the present
even as i read the newspapers or walk down the street looking
for it   and i pick up my hometown paper   the san diego
union and read about the grant hotel

now the grant hotel used to be the only tall
building in san diego   it wasnt very tall   it was about
ten stories tall   but for a long time it was the tallest
building in sleepy san diego   there are a lot of taller
ones now   but for a certain kind of businessman clientele
its had a kind of nostalgia and chic and was considered good
for christmas and new years parties and the like   though in

the last couple of years it had gotten quite a bit rundown
and a new ownership had just taken it over and was planning
to spruce it up

                        and whether in line with this or not   the
other day they were testing the hydraulic lift for the
outside fire escape   the mechanism failed and the falling
   fire escape killed an eighty-five year old man named angel
aquinero and his seventy-five year old friend sam marino who
happened to be walking by   and narrowly missed two
twenty-two year olds who scampered out of the way

                                                    and while i
find the whole story interesting   i find it curious that
the name of one of the fast twenty-two year olds was jack
   kemp   the same name as the distinguished supply side
legislator who had been a fleet footed quarterback behind one
of the worst offensive lines for the buffalo bills   where
   he had distinguished himself also for getting the hell out
of the way in a hurry   and i imagine if the policies he
has advocated result in a collapse he will once again be
   distinguished for getting the hell out of the way in a hurry
   or a lot quicker than any elderly retired cook

                        and i asked myself as i was reading the paper
   how come this fire escape being tested right in the middle
of the day on broadway fell on two street smart old men just
like that   didnt they have any ropes or some sort of barrier
and signs warning people away   no says the newspaper article
   there were no ropes or barriers or signs because theres
   no ordinance requiring them for testing the hydraulic lift
of a fire escape
                        well i suppose not   perhaps theyd never
had trouble before   but then had they had much experience
testing it   had they ever tested it before   did they test
it regularly   once a year maybe or just suddenly now
   because they were renovating and a city agency had just
noticed them and required the test   but there was nothing
about this in the paper either   still the paper mentioned
two men in street clothes shouting people away

                                                    now i have an
image of angel aquinero eighty-five years old his hearing

not so terribly good any more   concentrating on talking to
   his friend and listening to him while walking by   and
   when they shout at him he has things on his mind   more
   important than anything two punk kids could be calling out
waving rudely at him and samuel marino   and he's got a life
   to live angel   its his street   and the people of the
street recognize this by calling him the mayor the mayor of
   broadway   and i would think that the mayor of broadway
   deserves more consideration when he's walking down his own
street   than to be yelled at and have a fire escape fall on his
   head   but the hotel feels justified   because it was
operating within ordinances that didnt recognize the dignity
   due the mayor
                       and as i continued leafing through the
   newspaper looking for the present   i came on some letters
   relating to the problems of the tradition in the columns of
dear abby   two letters   while i was sitting in the plane
   thinking about the problems of the avant-garde   that from
two utterly distinct perspectives raised the problems posed
   by the present to the tradition
                                      one letter could have been
      written by harold bloom

                        "dear abby"   it went   "i am
   planning to marry this summer   my parents are divorced and
   my mother is remarried   i have my heart set on having a
   traditional church wedding   who should give me away?   my
      father or my stepfather?   both consider me their daughter
and i love them both equally   my mother says the one who
   pays for the wedding should have the right to give me away
probably my stepfather   this is giving me an ulcer   i've
   even considered eloping so i wouldnt have to make a choice
      but i really do want a church wedding
                                               i have a twenty-one
year old brother who could walk me down the aisle but he says
he'd rather be an usher
                          please tell me what to do   i dont
   want to hurt any feelings on my wedding day"

      but there is a second letter from a totally
   different point of view   and if the first one is harold

                                                    55

bloom   the second is a little more like me   this letter
is from a second wife who writes to console a writer of a
   previous day who had complained of the problems of being a
second wife

                              "dont despair   im also a number
two   the man i married was previously married to a
delightful woman named sue   for years my mother-in-law
   called me sue   my name is joan   she even gave me gifts
   on sues birthday   she loved sue and she loves me too
      now im divorced and my ex is presently going with a lady
named jean   i understand that my former mother-in-law is
   now calling jean joan
                         joan"

         so you can see why for me   joan   the tradition
   will resolve itself in the present   and all you have to do
is find it   but if you dont it will find you   often quite
rapidly and without warning   but in any case my feeling is
   that it will come as it came to me one day recently

               not long ago i moved my mother to san diego
      from brooklyn where she had lived for many years   now
   its a long distance from brooklyn to san diego   and the
   life thats lived here is as different as the climate   and i
   would never have moved her but her life was falling apart
         or at least she felt that it was   she was getting
older   she was seventy-eight or seventy-nine   and the
   neighborhood that she'd been living in for the last twenty
years   ocean parkway   had been running down and was now
   inhabited by strangers   who she felt were menacing and
strange   and she was finding it progressively more
      difficult to manage her daily affairs   putting her
checks in the bank and taking care of the gas bill and the
   telephone and the rent   so i moved her to an apartment
   in pacific beach near the bay   and i cant really manage
   her affairs very well   but even i can manage them better
than she can

               and i arranged to move her things from brooklyn and
flew out to get her   and i installed her in this sunny
little apartment on la playa in a small complex of apartments

56

managed by a very helpful and authoritarian ex-military man
who looked out for her and took her shopping when he could and
called me when he couldnt   and all seemed to be going
   fairly well
                    till she began to have problems with the
telephone company and san diego gas and electric   with whom
she quarreled over the bills even when i arranged to pay
   them   and with the bank   that she was convinced was
defrauding her of her interest   so that she went there
every day to make sure it was recorded   and fought with the
   tellers when they wouldnt satisfy her   and it got so that
the tellers would go to great lengths not to have to deal
with her   because from their point of view she would fly
   into inexplicable rages over matters they didnt understand
   and the sight of a little white haired lady in a small
brimmed orange cloche hat coming through the doors of their
   bank would strike terror into their hearts   and the more
attentive of them catching sight of her coming through the
doors clutching her ancient purse to her chest and holding a
bundle of bankbooks in her hand would beat it quickly to the
john or the coffee machine for a much needed break
                    and the manager would eventually call me and i
would have to drive down with her to straighten things out
while they listened   sympathetically and i tried to explain
   to her what they had quite correctly done   which only made
her angrier because they appeared to be talking to me instead
of to her   "and its my money" she said

              but all this was manageable until she started to
quarrel with her apartment manager or until she started to
suspect him   as she suspected everyone else   of stealing
   from her   her money her bankbooks her toothbrush her
needles and thread   and finally her ice cube trays

              at this point i moved her out into an apartment
   hotel   a resident hotel for elderly men and women where
they got their meals cooked and served to them their rooms
   cleaned and beds made   and lived with other men and women
whose capabilities were not much greater than their own
              which she might have enjoyed   except that she was
losing her grip on the present so that it didnt mean much to

her   and she complained of it for reasons that seemed odd
when she explained them to me

                                        they were prejudiced against
her because she was jewish   because she was from scranton
    and she wanted to go back to where her people were   in
new york   and it was useless for me to explain to her that
nearly thirty percent of the people that lived in her hotel
were jewish   that i'd heard them speaking yiddish and i'd
heard her speaking with them   and that her good friend
with whom i'd seen her sitting much of the time was italian
    but she spoke yiddish too   better than my mother who
was really a native speaker of english with a pennsylvania
accent   who had never really learned to speak a fluent
yiddish at all

          but what good would it do   all she wanted to do
was go home to the scranton of seventy years ago or the new
york of thirty or forty or fifty years ago   so i reminded
her that all of her remaining relatives were living in
miami now and maybe she would like to visit them   but that
worried her because her sister bessie would be nearly ninety
now and sarah must be over eighty-five   and sylvia   well
sylvia

          but i had an idea   i would call her brother
irving who was younger than she was   he was taking care of
sylvia and living in florida not far from her other sisters
    she could visit with him and get a chance to see sarah
and bessie before they died   and sylvia too   and the idea
of being with her family again her sisters and brother
    appealed to her because it was her only idea of home   so
i said that i would call irving because i thought she could
manage a plane trip if i put her on the plane at one end and
her brother picked her up at the other

                                        and i was about to do
this   when i got a phone call picked up the receiver and
heard a hoarse voice that sounded like a member of the mafia
or an italian bookie   that i recognized as my uncle irving
saying "hello david"

          now i hadnt heard that voice for years   but this

gentle heavy man spoke with the voice of a heavy   there
may be something about a persons life that brings one into
the world as a heavy   maybe running a candy store
surrounded by bookies and detectives he had come to sound
like one of them   developing over the years that kind of
cracked and breathy pharyngeal growl that i immediately
recognized as my uncle

              "hello irving" i said with a confidence
that surprised me but not him   though i had not spoken to
him for nearly twenty years
              and he said "listen sonny   i
know youre taking care of your momma"   i said "well she's
all right   shes not bad" i said   "she's in a hotel and
she's not too happy because she's not surrounded with family
  but shes comfortable"
              he said "look i know your momma is a
difficult person   she's never been very happy and i know
youre doing your best for her   but she's had a very hard
life   and i think it would do her good to come down here
and visit with her family"   i said thats a wonderful idea
how should we arrange it   and he says   "look she takes
the plane to fort lauderdale   i come in and pick her up
right away and she'll live the life of reilly"

    "the life of reilly"   i hadnt heard that
expression in years   since i was a kid and william bendix
played it on the radio in the nineteen forties   and my
uncle irving was promising my mother a rerun in the nineteen
eighties
          he said "yeah she'll lead the life of reilly   its
beautiful here   we'll take her all around she'll see the
seashore   she'll see all the children and grandchildren the
beautiful houses they live in   she'll live like a queen"

     i said "it sounds good   but why dont you call
her and talk to her too   itll do her good to hear your
voice and give her confidence   she may be a little nervous
about such a long trip"

       "sure sonny i understand   but maybe you should
give her my number too in case i cant reach her right away

ive got kind of irregular hours   im working as a night
watchman   and sometimes i'm not in"

              sure i said   ok irving   but i knew she'd
never be able to make the call   though i coached her on
how to do it from the pay phone in the hall   by dialing the
  operator and billing the call to me   because i knew that
she'd lose her confidence or forget altogether   but i said
sure and a week went by   two weeks   three weeks   no
  irving   and i couldnt figure out why irving hadnt called
in all that time

              so i asked my mother did you try to call
  irving   and this was a very difficult if not entirely
pointless thing to do   because having a conversation with
my mother about some specific act or event that either did
or did not occur in the recent past was difficult   because
of the way she loses hold of the present about as soon as it
  goes past   and pointless because what she says is so
  unreliable as she tries to cover up her losses   but i
tried to find out whether irving had called her   or more
improbably   whether she had called him   and she tried to
remember   or more precisely to answer   so we both tried
  and became exhausted with our effort

          she felt spent with the immense effort of
struggling with an uncooperative long distance operator who
refused to put her through   with a signal that didnt lead
to a familiar voice at the other side   and ended in tears
    for weeks she had been trying to get irving she had
called again and again   she was exhausted with all of the
  trying she was describing   and still there was no irving
and now she was close to tears because something might be
wrong

              and while i didnt really believe this i decided to
  call   so i dialed him in the morning and nobody answered
      i tried again in the afternoon and that night and the
next morning   and i remember thinking it was strange
      because i knew that his wife fanny stayed home much of
the time looking after my aunt sylvia who had become
something of an invalid and spent all of her days on the

60

couch looking at whatever was on television   so i thought
it was strange and kept on trying   and one day several
weeks later i dialed the number and somebody picks up the
phone and its a womans voice   and i say "hello   can i
speak with irving"   and the womans voice becomes hard and
cold and says "is this some kind of joke"   and i say "no
no   fanny is that you?"   she says   "david?   is that
you"   i said yes   and she said "irving died"   "what
happened?" i said

she said   "remember he called you?"
"yes"   "well that night he went to work at his
watchmans job   he went out to get a cup of coffee during
his break and a car came around the corner and hit him and he
got killed"

now i hadnt counted on the presence of fort
lauderdale or miami   or my uncle   who had appeared on the
telephone and then disappeared   nothing within the horizon
of my discourse could have prepared me for that moment with
my aunt fanny   who had just lost the husband she'd lived
with for over forty years and was now on the telephone

and it seems to me that if you cant respond to that
youre not in the avant-garde

the memphis art institute was a sleepy little art
school some of whose more energetic teachers got the idea of
exposing their mostly painting and sculpture students to a
range of art possibilities and they got a grant to bring in a
series of visiting artists from around the country   an
art historian   a soft spoken woman a native of memphis
took on the responsibility of getting me settled and showed
me around   the school was at the edge of a little park and
they had arranged for my lodging in a genteel old age home
close by   most of whose mindless residents were elderly
white folk tended by elderly blacks

when she picked me up she explained that they had
gotten my name from the LIST   a catalog of potential
visitors put together by an association of independent
curators   they had already had john baldessari yvonne
rainer and a traditional storyteller and she wondered a
little apologetically whether my work was like any of the
others   i thought for a moment and suggested it might be
something like the storytellers
she showed me the hall where
my performance was going to be   a school auditorium with a
raised stage which happened to have on it in addition a
speakers lectern   a blackboard a small round formica table
and two stools of different heights   all of which they were
going to clear away   but i asked her to leave them where
they were   just to take away the speakers lectern and
leave me some chalk for the blackboard   which she arranged
and then volunteered to show me around the city in which she
had been born and lived most of her life   and that

according to her was in an even more depressed state than the
rest of the country in reagans 1981 recession   the cotton
market was long gone   most of the industry had fled   the
black people were nearly all out of work and a lot of the
white working class

                          she showed me boss crumps dilapidated old
mansion   a relic from memphis' grand old wicked days   and
a view of the mississippi from the bluffs above   which she
said always made her a little sad   the city was doing a
major renovation on the buildings along the waterfront to
evoke the old sporting houses and riverboat entertainments
in the hopes of attracting a tourist trade to upscale
restaurants and fashionable boutiques   memphis used to be a
major cotton market she said and a rail center for lumber
and agricultural produce from all over the south   but the
plague of the 1870s killed off a large part of its
population   and though the city built itself up again
afterward   it never quite recovered   she looked down the
river a little wistfully

                       "we could have been atlanta" she said

durations

       as a performer im an improviser   so i dont know
exactly what im going to say when i begin   though ive
thought about talking of particular things   and when ive
  finished talking i may still be interested in something ive
said and i may want to think about it again   and sometimes
i'll want to look at it and i'll transcribe it and maybe even
publish it   in a more or less extensive form that hangs
  pretty close to the original talk or the sense of it
    even when ive extended it   because im much less
interested in revision and polishing than in the difference
between print and performance

                         now both are available and
  interesting for the representation of experience
  performance is attractive for its immediacy and power
  print for its continuing availability   which is a
convenience though sometimes delusory   because it seems to
promise so much clarity and duration   and i have an
attraction to clarity though not so much to duration   but
i have a much greater attraction to performance   to the
  moment   to that kind of performance in which the moment
directs me which way to go   the moment of addressing people
  who have come to hear me though they may not know me but
  have some expectation of what theyre going to hear

                                i know
that if i come here i was selected at least from some casual
  acquaintance with my name   drawn most likely from a list
  of similar names   and in fact it was a list called
  "the list"   and included a whole range of people in
the arts who are willing to travel about and do performances
or give lectures or simply present themselves and samples of

their work   and this set of performers and lecturers and
demonstrators includes a whole lot of very different people
     and thats all right   but im sure it reduces the
likelihood of your having very definite expectations of any
of us
          and i knew this before i came and i thought   i'll be
coming to an art school and ive taught in an art school
     but no ive never taught in an art school ive taught in a
university and thats not quite the same   but i taught in a
music school   once   for a year   i taught english in a
music school once by accident   i was replacing a friend of
mine who taught there regularly but got called away to
adapt a play for broadway   and it was at the last minute
and he was very responsible so he recommended me for the job

          now he taught two courses there   one was a course
in english composition   that was only a little mad
     teaching people who had no great desire to learn it how
to write english in a more or less comfortable and lucid way
that would not get them laughed at by other people who could
read
          since most of my students were musicians   not all of
whom could read   they were not all inclined to laugh at the
same sorts of things my friend was   but as he was both
kindly and polite he never really laughed out loud at his
musician students laughable mistakes   he took them all in
     stride and pointed out politely only the worst ones   and
since i was filling in for him i did the same
                                        the other course
was a history of english literature that began with beowulf
and ended with joyce   this was a little more peculiar
because of the wide range of cultures and histories i was
supposed to teach   but i took it very seriously and each
week i prepared a careful lecture on the backgrounds and
styles of the beowulf poet and chaucer and william
shakespeare   and i remember one week preparing the first
couple of books of paradise lost   for which purpose i read
the whole epic over again and thought how wonderful it was
and bizarre for this great protestant poet to compose this
lush baroque and sensually catholic poem   and i was so

66

struck by the struggle between the language and the doctrine
that i prepared what i thought was a brilliant lecture on
 this extravagant   michelangelesque   poem   and thought
about it all the way on my ride in to mannes college on the
 elevated of the pelham bay line from where i happened to be
  living at that time   in the house of a dentist art
collector who was away travelling in the far east acquiring
art while i was living in his buddha filled house on benson
street in the south bronx near the whitestone bridge

          and as it happened it was snowing that day
        snowing hard as the train passed over the little houses
of italian workmen   filling their little gardens with snow
high enough to cover the small statues and the barren
rosebushes wrapped in tarpaper and even the rocks of the
little grottoes and as i watched the snow fall i thought what
a great lecture im going to give on this renaissance image
maker and this sistine chapel of a poem   but when i made my
way up madison avenue to my classroom in mannes college only
one member of my class had arrived   a lovely japanese girl
    a violinist who spoke nearly no english at all
                                          and as i
    stared into the hopeful face of my only student   that was
as beautiful and flat and pale as a japanese print i lost all
hope of milton and the renaissance and that tortured diction
  and we talked im not sure how for hours about winter and
  those japanese houses that are so lovely to look at with
their elegant shojis and fusumas but so cold that you have to
  wear padded clothing all the time that your legs are
cramping from kneeling on those neat little tatamis while you
  contemplate the chilly splendor of your house   so that its
not surprising that if youre a violinist and a woman   and
  can afford it   you may want to leave those beauties for a
  steam heated apartment in manhattan   and a professional
concert career
                    and it was something like that she talked about
  somehow while i listened and realized that there are some
things you simply cannot prepare for

            but i was thinking on the way here that i was
  coming to an art school and i thought i had some idea of what

art schools were like   because i'd been around art schools
even if i'd never taught in one   i'd visited art schools in
lots of places   and in my experience art schools are more
like other art schools than theyre not   and the people who
come to art schools are more like each other than theyre like
other people   and even though this was an art school in
memphis   a town i knew nothing about aside from the history
of egypt or life on the mississippi   i still had the
feeling i knew generally what to expect

because most people
in art schools are interested in making objects   and im
surely not interested in making objects   but i could think
about why people are interested in making objects   i'd
thought about it before   and it seemed to me that most of
the people in art schools who are interested in making
objects   want to have the feeling that theyre making
meaningful objects   they seem to want to make objects that
mean something   because if they dont mean anything   those
people dont think of those objects as art   but perhaps if
theyre beautiful enough or well enough made   as the objects
of some kind of craft

now this may not be the best way to talk about it
but most of the people who want to make objects that they
think of as art want to make objects that are meaningful in
something like the way an utterance is meaningful   but
there is something of a difficulty in this   in that talk
seems to disappear into its meaning in the minds of its
hearers   while an object   once it leaves the hands of its
maker   tends to remain somewhere between its maker and any
potential receiver   and it is this capacity of objects to
remain that resists their dissolution into meaning

now i know
that it is also this potential of objects for duration that
is part of their attraction   both for the people who want
to make them and the people who want to perceive them   this
tenacious physical hold   on existence   which gives an
artist a kind of claim on human attention   over a period of
time that is a promise   both for its makers and perceivers
of a type of survival   in this duration

68

                                             and this is
something we all experience as artists   because even
as a poet and a performer   which for me is nearly the same
thing   i want to do something that will have all the
   immediacy and impact of a wisecrack   and yet will offer
itself up to the mind again and again like a koan   and stay
long enough for that   which is a kind of duration

        so i can understand how you may want to make
something that will offer itself up again and again to
   experience   something that will yield with each contact
      maybe over time   a whole set of related experiences
maybe rich and mysterious and new   and i can sympathize
with that desire   but somehow that desire has gotten mixed
up   as you obviously know   with the idea of how long an
   object might conceivably last   and theres a history to
this lust after objects that might last forever   and its
not for nothing that a chatty roman poet wanted to brag that
his talk would outlast the monuments of marble or bronze
   and that many years later william shakespeare   who had
read this roman poet in school and was now writing some fast
   little fourteen liners   took courage from the fact that
some sixteen hundred years later   through whatever
accidents of education and transmission   he was still
   reading this roman poet and felt moved to translate this
great brag and repeat it about a poem of his own

      "not marble nor the gilded monuments of princes shall
   outlive this powerful rhyme"   which sounds very nice but
the key word here is "live"   that stands in a funny relation
to monuments as well as to talk   though its relation to
   monuments is surely funnier

           i was in france for a month last year between
november and december   i had some performances to do in
paris and normandy   i had an apartment there   it was very
   comfortable and convenient for working in with a sitting
room and tall windows   right at the edge of the left bank
on rue st julien le pauvre   and i had a view through the
windows of a little square and of notre dame that was just
   across the seine   and right across the street from me was

                                                    69

the church of st julien which was one of the oldest churches
in paris   but i was there for work and spent most of my
  free time with friends   except for a brief look into st
julien

        one sunny morning after breakfast i strolled across
  the street where they were digging up the old cobblestones
with jackhammers and replacing them with new ones   smooth
cut rock slabs that must have been much bigger than the old
ones   and much less suitable for throwing in the event of a
new revolution   and i went in through the depressing little
  facade that it turned out had replaced the old one when
they destroyed the portal and cut two bays off the nave to
prevent them from collapsing in the middle of the seventeenth
century
        the church was a dark melancholy little place   that
had had its heyday in the thirteenth and fourteenth centuries
when it was a grand priory ruled over by a cardinal priest
  and was the meeting place for several corporations and the
assemblies of the university of paris where the faculty
elected its rector magnificus   and this greatness got it
into trouble with a bunch of angry students who sacked it in
the sixteenth century as a protest against one such election
  from then on it went into decline   to a simple priory
  and then a dependent chapel of nearby st severin in the
seventeenth century   closing during the revolution and
turning into a salt warehouse during the empire   from which
it was restored to use as a church for the old hotel dieu
after 1826 and finally acquired some time after the
demolition of the old hospital by a melchite sect around
  1890
        in spite of the architectural butchery to which it had
been subjected   and the iconostasis of the eastern rite
    that blocked off part of its twelfth century choir
  its arcades and vaults still possessed the acoustic
resonance of their gothic construction   and it seemed to be
used now mainly for concerts of ancient music   and one
stroll around this glum little church was all of my
sightseeing till i was through with my performances   then
i announced to the lady who ran the shop where i regularly

bought my morning paper that i was through with my work and
ready to be the tourist   and i was even ready to visit the
   louvre   which she assured me was a valuable thing to do
because there was much of interest there for everybody

         and i suppose there is   and i went there and i
had in mind to look at the watteaus and the van loo portrait
 of diderot and the fragonards   maybe even go look for
bonington   but everywhere i went there were these coercive
signs pointing in the direction of leonardos mona lisa
      now im not in love with the whole italian renaissance
but if there is one painter i have nearly no interest in at
all its leonardo   who was certainly an interesting man
     and whose journals i have read many times with great
 pleasure   wondering over the details of his lethal
imaginings of tanks and submarines and poison gas and his
 endless fascination with water   but his paintings are
   another matter   and the mona lisa may be the most typical
         i had never seen it except in reproduction and i
   had no desire to see it   even when it came to new york i
   had resisted   though i got tied up in a traffic jam near
 the metropolitan because of it   and once having to pass on
 foot by way of the met   i found myself walking past a long
   line of people patiently waiting their turn to see it
      attended by an unusual number of peddlers good humor men
 bagel vendors and guys hustling helium filled balloons   as
   well as one seedy looking salesman hawking slick looking
   eight-by-ten color reproductions that were the closest i'd
 come to the celebrated painting   and one old man showing
 the print to his very little grandson smiling at it fondly
 and saying to no one in particular   "isnt she beautiful"

         so i ignored the signs and went to the watteaus
and bouchers and fragonards   that laid as little claim to
   duration as bubbles   and i worked my way past the le nains
      where all those decent peasants seem to have come
   forward at just that moment to have their pictures painted
   the way families on sunday in the park stand up in a group
 to have their photograph taken   and got to the van loo
   diderot and was confirmed in the truth of its charm that
      diderot thought something of a lie and blamed on the charm

of madame van loo who was making him laugh

but the signs were beginning to get me with their
insistent instructions toward leonardo   and i gave in and
went backward in time past the baroque the rembrandts and
entered the room with the three leonardos   and there behind
a velvet rope and behind glass was the handsome painting of
the fashionable italian lady smiling politely in front of
that weird northern landscape

this was the one that of all
ancient pictures time had dimmed the least?

there was a small
crowd of people in the room in front of me   grouped around
the easel of a painter who was copying la gioconda   and i
peered over their heads to see what he was making of it   he
had maintained the heart shaped face   slightly bobbed her
hair and snubbed her nose   turned up the mouth into a
perfectly lively little smile   and left no trace of
landscape

as i passed the rembrandts on the way out i
stopped for a moment to look once again at the self portrait
with the palette in his hand and the turban tied around his
head   which looks more like a painters cloth to protect his
hair   and an expression that suggests some kind of comment
on the object of painting its meaning and perhaps its duration
a comment that looks to me like the beginning of a very
rueful jewish grin   that expresses something of my own
disdain for the idea of duration

but this morning when i was setting out on my way
here   i had to get up early in the morning to be here in
time   my plane was leaving at seven-thirty   or it was
scheduled to leave then   and i had to get up about
five-thirty to have time enough for a shower and coffee and
the drive down to lindbergh field   and on the way down i
was thinking about these things but mainly about duration
the kind of duration that would mean something to me
and the duration i started to think about   as the
plane took off   was a kind of double duration

as the plane takes off from lindbergh airport on

its way east to places like dallas–fort worth it taxis out
past the marine training camp and heads west over the ocean
and then rolls in a leisurely circle back east again   and
as the plane took off and headed east i was settled in my
seat   which happened to be next to the window   because on
morning flights i like to look out occasionally at the
landscape   and i was waiting for the pilot to take off the
seat belt sign so i could lower my table and rest a book on
it   or maybe my newspaper   and i was sitting on the left
and glanced over at my neighbor on the right

          we had three seats in the row and an empty one
between us   because it was early morning and not very
crowded   and he was sitting there hunched forward reading a
book   a tall man   or maybe he only seemed so from the
way he was hunched forward   reading a serious book   which
from what i could make out   because there was an empty
seat between us   was a paperback of a saul bellow novel
     and he was a serious man reading a serious novel by a
serious novelist   though i couldnt make out which saul
bellow novel it was   and i was sitting there glancing idly
at my neighbor and at my own little black notebook   one of
those grainy black covered drawing books   and sketching
idly with my pencil   while i was actually thinking about
duration   the several kinds of duration   that i was being
exposed to at that moment

                    at that moment inside the plane i
was exposed to the duration of my neighbor reading saul
bellow and probably   waiting for his breakfast   as i was
drawing and waiting for my breakfast   thinking about
duration and looking out the window at the landscape passing
     below   and at that moment we were coming up over the low
foothills of the first mountain ranges on our way east   and
i was watching as we crossed the first ridge and i thought
aha were crossing the first one and soon were going to be in
a little trough and then we'll be crossing a second ridge and
then we'll be coming down into a desert   and what time will
it be then?   and i marked the time down in my notebook

          now the way for me to do this is to give you a
sense of the window that was on my left   and the windows

of an airliner are plastic and softly curved like a screen
on which things are continually coming up   and the aisle
    which was on my right   is a place where things are
also continually happening   stewardesses keep appearing
and making announcements and offering you things like soft
 drinks or peanuts or headphones   and i was looking out of
my soft little window out of which mountains were now
 appearing and i was wondering how long it had taken us to
 get here

        i figured we'd waited about ten minutes on the
 runway because the flights were slightly backed up   and
that was seven-forty   and i figured wed been flying for
 little more than ten minutes   say twelve   and were
passing over these craggy little hills   which then
disappear   and we must be on the other side of them because
 im looking at smaller hills that are then giving way to
relatively flat land   and i look out at the flat land and
 decide that must be near the salton sea   because the flat
land outside my window is some kind of settlement that is
 neatly laid out like the ground plan of a japanese house
into a set of tatamis

        and im thinking about the time   inside the plane
 and outside   and a stewardess comes by on the aisle and
wants to know whether i want an omelette or fruit filled
pancakes for breakfast   i debate this for a moment
    although i know which one is going to be worse   the
omelette will at least have eggs in it and what can they do
to eggs   while the fruit in the pancakes will probably be
canned and a little bit wonderful   like japanese paper
flowers with corn syrup poured over them   so i go with the
omelette   and the omelette comes while im still thinking
 about time   the amount of time it took them to get out the
omelette   while out my window the landscape is changing
again as the desert is going away and we start climbing
hills   little hills that start appearing on the other side
    and as i peer out in front of us little snow caps start
appearing and my omelette has arrived   in a funny form
    its rolled up tight like a yellow napkin   but theres
nothing inside it   only theres a little aluminum foil dish

74

containing the omelette materials   the tomatoes and onions
  and whatever else has been cooked into the omelette mix
     and i wonder what am i supposed to do to get the
omelette filler into the middle of my omelette   and i look
  at my breakfast tray and i figure i dont have the right
  equipment   but i take my fork and my knife and i try to
unroll the omelette   and i find out its not so much rolled
as cooked solid in the shape of a roll   theres some kind
  of flour or paste thats been cooked into it and wont ever
  unfold without maybe a surgical scalpel   so i figure what
im supposed to do is dump the filler on top of the egg and
  eat the inside of my omelette on the outside   and its
  having your breakfast in a different way
                                                                so i dump the
tomatoes and onions on top of my omelette and i look for my
  bread   because while im not a great bread eater i find
it hard to eat eggs without bread or toast   and i look for
it and its some kind of ugly looking sweet roll   but theres
  something rounded and brown on the other side of my omelette
     and i wonder is it fried fish?   this early in the
morning?   but this is an airliner and time is all different
  on airliners   i figure its some kind of potato goody and
i probe it with my fork   and under the crust it is some
kind of gelatinous white mass   a potato goody   i taste it
  and push it carefully to the other side of my tray   i pick
up my coffee and look out the window again

           now we're rising over real mountain terrain   and
inside the plane its getting colder   and this is happening
  very fast   how much time has been going by   its hard for
me to say   but weve been heading quickly into the mountains
while ive been slowly eating my breakfast   or as much of it
  as i could manage
                              and then suddenly im startled by something
inside of the plane   somewhere in back of me down the aisle
  on my right there is a little man standing and shouting
  "how dare you hit me with your tray"   and hes standing
  there practically hopping with rage and shouting at someone
who must be still sitting over there near the window on the
  right and not answering   and you know how it is on planes

youre in such a tight space that you try hard to ignore
anything close to you thats not neighborly   and everyones
looking at this stocky little man standing in the aisle and
shouting   and at the same time trying to ignore him and
hoping he will cut it out and sit down   but there is no
ignoring this fierce little man who is angrily repeating his
charge and something about an attaché case   while the man
he is yelling at is mumbling something from the window   and
one stewardess comes rushing up the aisle while another one
rushes down toward the cabin   and my neighbor looks up
from his novel   which must have been very absorbing
because he looks up somewhat abstracted and puzzled
so i explain someone is supposed to have hit the little
man with a tray and done something to his attaché case

"well surely it couldnt have been deliberate or it
seems very unlikely" says my neighbor   but the little man
certainly thinks it was deliberate and stands there
practically hopping on one leg in affronted anger demanding
an apology and challenging in a very threatening manner till
the pilot or copilot or navigator comes rushing up the aisle
and interposes his heavy body between the fierce little man
and his offender   and together with the stewardess pushes
him gently but surely into another seat on our side of the
aisle

and while this is going on and the copilot is
standing there talking to the angry little man i take the
opportunity to look at my neighbor   he's a well to do
business man in a conservative blue business suit with a
paisley print tie in a tight little knot under a sleeveless
pullover   a handsome man in his late sixties i think
from the graying hair and the drying skin of his
somewhat austere looking face

and we start talking   my neighbor and i   while
the stewardess is still standing beside the angry little man
and talking to him in softer tones while the landscape is
changing again   and were dropping out of the high mountains
and passing over a terrain that is arranged in small hills
like curious little folds in an otherwise flat tablecloth

76

and we're talking my neighbor and i

"i noticed that you were writing" he said "you have a
very fine hand   are you an engineer?"
    "no" i said "im a poet"   and he looked a little
depressed
    "i saw you drawing and i thought they were sine waves
are you going somewhere to give a reading?"
    he was an educated man   "no" i said "not a reading
exactly   a performance   at an art school in memphis"

    and as that seemed a little peculiar we got to
talking   he was himself a writer   of a kind   he wrote
books on military strategy   he had been a submarine
commander and now he wrote books on strategy   in fact he
had been involved in the mx missile dispute that he supposed
i'd heard about   and i had

        being a naval man   as he pointed out   he might
be somewhat biased but he favored a naval distribution of our
deterrent force   and he preferred submarine based missiles
to the mx   which he didnt think very wise or protectable
    even in hardened silos   which couldnt get enough
support because of the expense anyway   so he'd been trying
to persuade people that the mx was impractical and
uneconomical   he'd even tried to persuade his old friend
herman kahn   but as he admitted with a sigh herman just
    wasnt very interested   and most of his research contracts
were financed by the air force
                            my neighbor was an interesting
man and we talked for a while   having found out that i was
in literature he wanted to know what i thought of the english
department at the university of virginia   where his son
had gone to take a masters in literature after a b.a. at
    hawaii and a short stay at yale   and i didnt know much
about it   except that my old friend diane wakoski had once
taught and acquired an insignificant boy friend there   and
    bill seitz had gone to the art departrnent there when he
was dying and trying to get away from the real world   and
the english department had acquired charles wright   a nice
    bland poet   and they probably worried a lot about poetry

77

written in lines   but my heart wasnt in it   and he
started telling me how his son was now studying law and was
about to get a job in miami   which was a more exciting town
     while i continued to listen but was thinking of
something that had happened to me the night before

          and as i was listening to how my neighbors son had
chosen miami to live in because it was a growing city with
all sorts of colorful new groups of foreigners and legal
problems to work on i was thinking about my last evening in
san diego
          i had gone to the university library to pick up a
few books i needed   and elly   my wife   needed some
books for the new exhibition she was working on   she was
looking for pictures of ancient playing cards for a series
of emblematic paintings in a performance she was preparing
     and she came along with me   and we were working in
different parts of the library   but when i finished i went
down to find her   and she was still looking through stacks
of old books on tarot and playing cards   so i said look
i'll cut out now and start supper and when youre through you
can go back to the studio and drive home with blaise
          because it was beginning to get dark and elly   who
doesnt like to drive at night   could let our sixteen year
old son drive her back home   so i got in my van and drove
off
          and when i got home i turned on the radio   and while i
listened to the music i flipped through my books and started
to make supper   and an hour goes by and nobody arrives
          and i'm not an alarmist though this seems unlikely
because elly had only a little more looking to do and blaise
has homework   but i wait another half hour before i realize
that something is up and i call her studio   her assistant
is there   and russ tells me he hasnt seen elly since she
went off to the library and the last time he saw blaise
          an hour ago   he said they were on the way home

          and my neighbor is talking about living in san
diego where he was born   and bicycling around coronado
where he'd lived as a boy and how much he had loved it   but
how his wife whod been an off broadway actress and with whom

he'd lived in hawaii and virginia now near washington   when
theyd visit now and then and stay on shelter island   would
wonder what there was to do in san diego and how anyone could
live there
                and i was thinking how i was living out in our
arroyo in the sagebrush among the rabbits and quail and
coyotes and our three dogs   and how i was beginning to get
worried because it was two hours now since i'd left eleanor
        and i determined that there was nothing to worry about
        because if anything had happened it was sure to be less
serious than anything i could imagine   and resolving not to
think about it i got up and walked out onto the deck and
looked down into the valley below   because i live at the
top of this wash   which makes it the top of a hill   from
   which i can look out and see the ocean a couple of miles to
the west and the lights of la jolla and san diego more miles
to the south
                and i looked out and i walked around the clearing
in front of our house   followed by our three dogs who
thought it was strange for me to just be walking around out
there and not feeding them at this time or not doing
   something else useful inside   because in our domestic
arrangement its my son blaise who cares for and feeds the
dogs while i do the cooking and elly does the dishes   and
they were also probably surprised at elly and blaise not
being home   so they kept following me around whimpering and
whining a little   and i'm looking out at the stars and
wondering whether i should go back in and start feeding the
dogs when the phone rings   and i have a feeling that
something is going on and rush back in to answer it but it
   stops   and i begin to worry
                        and all this time my neighbor
is telling me about coronado in the thirties and then living
in hawaii and how colorful it is   compared to san diego
   because of all of those different ethnic groups   like
the japanese and chinese   and how there werent many in san
diego then   which was just a sleepy navy town   but fun
for a kid growing up in all that empty land   though he
   thought that now it must be beginning to change   with the
vietnamese people coming in after the war   and the

university and all that building that was going on   which
   for him was still new   though he comes back with his wife
to visit every few years
                         and i agreed that it was getting more
interesting now   while i was still thinking of standing out
on our deck where i'd gone back out and was waiting to find
out what had happened to my wife and my son because i didnt
want to simply sit around inside the house being nervous
      and i looked over to the lights of the university
library some six miles away   till the phone rang again and
i dashed in to answer   and it was eleanor calling to tell
me that   the car had died on the small empty road near the
hospital and had to be towed to the shell station near the
foot of our valley   and i rushed down to the shell station
      where elly told me how the car had just coughed
sputtered and then gone dead on the road   and i remembered
that in the capri the gas gauge had almost never worked so i
asked elly   are you sure you set the odometer   "you mean
the button i always push the mileage button when i fill the
tank"   and i said "what if you forgot?"   and i went over
and kicked the car body near the gas tank and it sounded
hollow   so we filled the tank and drove back up the hill

         now all the time this was happening i was in the
airplane talking about san diego and hawaii and the
university of virginia   and about saul bellow   because my
neighbor was telling me about the book he'd been reading
      which turned out to be about bellow and his wife   who
is really a mathematician but in this book is an astronomer
      and i knew this only because my school was trying to
hire the two of them   but bellow loved chicago and was not
willing to give it up for san diego at this time of his life
      any more than my neighbors wife would be willing to give
up virginia for san diego or than elly or i would be willing
to give up san diego for new york or chicago   or london or
paris after all the living we had done in it
                              and as we walked
out of the plane together into the dallas–fort worth airport
   past the security policemen who had come to detain the two
quarreling passengers   i had the sense of a duration   or

several durations   that i could understand   and ive
attempted to describe it in such a way so that you could
understand it too   but as i think about it i realize that
i have experienced it only as long as ive been telling it
     and ive been telling it for what seems like a long time
of twenty minutes or so   while i lived it for three hours
or more   but as i go on living this duration will get
shorter and shorter   as i think of it next month or next
year   and i may be able to summarize it in my mind in a
matter of seconds   till maybe i lose it altogether as an
image   and it contracts to the point where it will hide
behind a phrase or a name from which i can only call it up
by chance   with the right password and then only in the
act of a telling that may turn it into a quite different
experience and duration
                              but if this is true of this experience
     which was not especially pointed or important   it may
be true of all other experiences as well   and then how much
of our life do we possess as its parts slip away so casually

                    earlier this week   last monday i went to
visit my mother and my mother-in-law   theyre both elderly
ladies in their seventies and they live in a place called
collwood villa   a residential hotel in east san diego that
looks after them a little   prepares meals for them sees
that their rooms are cleaned and organizes a number of
things for them to do during the day if they feel like it
     films and classes and lectures and bingo games   it was
the fourteenth of february and scotty the social director had
arranged a valentines day party   to which we were invited
          and as usual we were late
                              the party was scheduled for
six-thirty and elly had stopped into pirets   a high class
san diego épicerie to buy two boxes of fancy french candies
for the ladies so that we got there at seven   but the party
was also late   the kitchen staff were still cleaning up
the dining room after the early supper   and scotty with the
help of a few of the maintenance people   was trying to get
the party room ready   the party room was in the other
building and there was a lot of noise and confusion as the

help carried chairs and trays from one place to the other
while the old people   confused by all this bustle
   wandered around the lobby or walked tentatively into the
music room   or simply stood in the corridor aimlessly
 watching the goings on

              my mother was standing in the doorway of the music
lounge   a small white haired woman in a pink cardigan and
pink slacks   and when she saw me she started to cry   so i
went up to her and put my arm around her and asked   "what
are you crying for ma" as i watched the large tears roll
down her cheeks   because she was really sobbing now

         "i thought you had abandoned me" she wailed
         "what made you think that"
         "i thought you had deserted me   rejected me" she
continued as i tried to comfort her by stroking her hair
         "whyd you think that?" i repeated
         "i dont know   probably because i like to hurt
myself" she said as the weeping continued
         "why is that?"
         "because thats what im like" she answered proudly
and abruptly stopped weeping as she noticed my mother-in-law
who had just wandered in from the corridor where she had been
standing aimlessly
         "look jeanette" she called out "the children are
here"   and my mother-in-law   a beautiful little dark
haired lady   smiled sweetly and a little vaguely out of her
lovely dark eyes   first at my mother and then at us
         "are they supposed to be   molly?"   and elly
rushes up and embraces jeanette and says   "yes were
supposed to be   its valentines day mother and theres a
party today"
                   and jeanette smiles and turns to my mother "you
hear molly?   thats wonderful"
                        and elly immediately gives
them the little boxes of french candy   which are gift
wrapped in gold paper with a silver ribbon tied around them
   that both of the ladies have trouble opening and want to
know whats inside   so elly goes up and opens them and says
         "its candy and its for both of you for valentines day"

82

and we show them the little silver wrapped candies
that they look at rather vaguely   and i ask   "wheres
the party?"

            "party?   is there a party?"   and i see some
people heading off in what i take to be the direction of the
party room   so i grasp my mother under the arm and elly
takes hers and we head off in the direction of the traffic

    and on the way down the corridor we encounter a little
old polish lady whos been standing there not knowing where
to go and she asks us where we are going
                                        i say
to the party the valentines day party and i take her arm and
    bring her with us   this pudgy little old polish lady who
wants to know if there will be dancing   "oh if theres a
    party i hope therell be dancing   i love dancing"   and i
say there probably will be dancing and also champagne   and
    she says "i hope there will be dancing   i love dancing"

        and as i look back down the corridor i see
that my wife whos been leading her mother down the corridor
has found a little mexican lady who wants to know where
theyre going   and when she finds out its to a party a
    valentines day party she is also pleasantly surprised and
comes along with them as we make our way into a large room in
    the other building   where a lot of tables and chairs have
been set up between a makeshift counter   behind which
several workers are filling up plastic glasses with champagne
and loading little paper plates with clusters of colorful
cookies and petits fours   and a large open space that would
probably serve as the dance floor
                                    we got the ladies seated at
one of the tables and elly went up to get them some cookies
while i went to get the champagne   and on my way up to the
counter i noticed   at a table on the other side of the
room a small bubbly company of spanish
people   one a small dark haired woman with very high heels
    her hair drawn up in a kind of high top knot under a comb
and wearing a mantilla   was talking in a bubbly spanish to
    a stolid sandy haired man in a pale blue suit holding a
guitar   so that i realized there would be dancing spanish

dancing and returned with the glasses of champagne for
the six of us   but it turned out that my mother and the
little polish lady didnt like champagne   so i went back to
get them some fruit juice

and it was taking a while for
things to get started   scotty was leaning over the table
with the company of dancers   she was bringing them
champagne and talking with them while the guitarist was
tuning his guitar   and etta   the manager of collwood
villa   an enormous woman in a pink square shouldered suit
with a fur trimmed collar was standing on the dance floor
talking to a tall workman looking guy in a pale amber suit
who was slowly and absent-mindedly stroking her prodigious
ass   till at some point she laughed and dismissed him
turned to the people who were almost all in their seats
now   and thanked everyone who had helped in the
preparations for the festivities   and announced that this
year we were going to have a program of flamenco dancing and
music   when suddenly this little flock of quick moving
spanish people burst onto the dance floor clicking and
gabbling like a bunch of bright little geese

there were four of them and the guitarist   who
had seated himself toward the rear and was still tuning up
his guitar   and another man who i thought was probably the
singer but spent most of the time standing alongside of the
guitarist clapping out rhythms   and the three women   the
fierce looking dark haired professional with the sideburns
and mantilla and comb   who looked as if she must have
danced night clubs in las vegas   a taller red headed woman
with a plunging neckline and heavy makeup and the kind of
skirt that when you flip it up it shows your legs and
ruffles in front   and with these two younger women who were
probably both in their thirties   there was another older
one a tiny plump person of nearly seventy with rakishly
curved side locks electrical energy and a laughing little
face
and as they burst onto the stage the little polish lady
said once again "i hope were going to have dancing i dont
want to just sit around and eat"   and i explained that we

84

were first going to have flamenco dancing by the señora
alvarez whom etta had announced   and the dancing had
started already   the little one was clicking her castanets
and clapping along with the standing man   the dark haired
professional had raised her arms over her head and was
stamping her heels and flirting professionally with the red
headed one   who was looking somewhat dykey now taut and
slim as a foil with her elbows held close to her body as she
circled an imaginary handkerchief with small percussive steps
while the dark haired one raised her fan and clicking her
castanets slowly   inclined toward her partner as the
standing man emitted a soft wailing sound

    "are we having a party" asked jeanette   "yes" i
say "its a terrific party isnt it jeanette?   theres even
champagne"   and she says "is there champagne?   i think
i'd like some champagne"   and i point out that she has
some in front of her   and she looks at it and says "i do?"
and she drinks it and smiles while my mother explains that
she doesnt like champagne or alcohol of any kind   but
jeanette tells her she should try some because its really
good   and my mother takes a little sip out of my glass and
makes a horrible face
          "i just dont like alcohol" she says
"not even passover wine and thats much sweeter than this"
          "you should try some a little wine is
good for you molly" says jeanette   but my mother shakes
her head and smiles contentedly   "i never liked it and i
never will   thats just what im like"

    meanwhile the dance has become a kind of conflict
courting dance   the dancers have turned their backs to each
other and the dark haired one is clicking her castanets in
sharp little bursts answered by the heels of the dykey one
    and their two backs arched away from each other make a
tense little bow seemingly stroked by the husky voice of the
male singer   who together with the tiny older one is
clapping his hands generally inciting the dancers   and i
say "jeanette its just like cabaret night at maudes"   the
hotel she ran for years in upstate new york where half of
juilliard and the singers and dancers and violinists that

made the summer hotel circuit sang and danced and played
but she looked at me blankly as if she'd forgotten
   and the dark haired dancer had swung back in front of
her partner now and was magnetizing him with her fan
   drawing him forward   the red haired woman   with
clicks and heel taps   and the red headed one was coming
close to her now   putting his arm around her and feeling
her up a little   which she allowed for a bit   before
moving regretfully away

         it was real spanish dancing   without andalusian
duende maybe but with a kind of style   the guitarist and
the male singer   what need would they have of the dark
andalusian powers or of deep song?   and the dark haired
dancer?
         but the dykey woman is singing now and the older
woman is dancing   the red headed woman has a deep hoarse
contralto   and she's saying something low and suggestive
in a spanish i cant quite make out   and theyre all clapping
their hands as the little one is dancing now   and she is an
almost globular little person with a cheerful face and she's
wearing a very long aqua gown with a tight skirt that has a
slit   which rises half way up the calf and a plunging
neckline from which her plump bosom is always threatening
to be emerging   and she does a wonderful drawing of a dance
   that she keeps stepping into and out of   and to which
she keeps referring with the castanets that she clicks with a
fierce éclat   and that she keeps affirming and denying
with her wicked little grin
                           and sometimes she smiles
seductively   and it is truly seductive and you believe it
because her body carries her into her dance for a step or
two as she flips back the skirt and displays the trim curve
of an ankle   or preens for a little to exhibit the solidity
of her hip or the soft curve of her breast by raising her
arm   before she withdraws from it with a laugh   this
drawing of a dance that she does and doesnt do   while the
guitarist draws arabesques around her and the singer
punctuates each entry with some raucous contralto comment
   because this sexy little dancer is seventy years old and

looks like a vigorous french concierge
and then the dark
haired professional the main dancer is rested and returns
and the singer takes on a more consistently raucous tone
the audience starts helping out with the clapping and
the dancer takes her long shawl and tries to coax a member
of the audience out onto the floor with it
the first one she
tries is a respectable looking gentleman probably somebodys
relative   and she loops the shawl around his waist and
tries to dance him out onto the floor but he is awfully
embarrassed and keeps shaking his head diffidently   hoping
to be released while she plays seductively with him and
rolls her eyes and sways   which only makes him more
embarrassed   and some of the old people laugh including my
mother   though jeanette doesnt pay much attention
and at
this moment   etta the boss of the whole establishment
who is one tough cookie   has found herself a great big
red jacket that is from some kind of doormans outfit and has
huge padded and gold braided shoulders   and comes dancing
out onto the floor in her version of a spanish dance holding
a huge blood red valentines heart that gets everyone
laughing enough to give the shy gentleman sufficient cover
to escape to his seat and allow the dancer to search for a
more willing candidate
and she finds one   in the first row
and its my wife eleanor who is really a dancer or had
been a dancer   a modern dancer and a folk dancer but not a
flamenco dancer   and elly grins and shrugs and the crowd
cheers her on as she follows the dark haired professional
spanish dancer out onto the floor with everyone including
her mother laughing and clapping their hands and cheering
her on   and she's dancing a somewhat different kind of
dance   more like a russian two step than flamenco   which
is what the dark haired one is dancing   but they are both
couple dances   preening and strutting percussive dances
and the two women are cheerfully and energetically
circling each other flirting and arching their backs and
stamping their feet and throwing back their heads   one in

the russian manner and the other in the spanish   with
enough conviction for you to expect one or the other of them
to cry out a spanish olay and russian hai to the delight of
the musicians who are seriously clapping them on while the
audience is cheering and jeanette observes to no one in
particular "it was always like this at maudes" and my mother
asks "what is this little box here?" and i explain that its
the candy that elly and i have brought her for valentines
day   at which jeanette discovers her box and wants to know
what it is   so i explain all over again that it contains
valentines day candies and they are for her to eat   and to
save if she wants to take them to her room   and maybe she'd
like to taste one now and perhaps give some to her friends
the little mexican lady and the little polish lady   and she
looks across the table at the two ladies and smiles and then
discovers the box again and asks whats this   and i reply
that its candy valentines day candy   and she wants to know
where did she get it and i tell her again and she looks very
happy   "thats so sweet thats so sweet" she says "im so
happy youre here"   and she was very happy and started to
cry and i ask her why are you crying and she says "because
im happy"

        now the dancing was over   the dancers had returned
to their seats and eaten and had their champagne and gone
    the crowd at the tables had begun to thin out as people
    got up to leave and wandered off down the corridor and into
the lobby where relatives were taking their leaves   and a
few of the old people had gone back into the music room
    where a number of others who had not been to the party
were sitting on sofas listening to a white haired lady who
must have been a church organist once playing the piano while
a younger and much handsomer woman was singing in a pure and
gorgeous soprano with many graceful flourishes golden
oldies from the twenties like "when irish eyes are smiling"
"let me call you sweetheart" and "you are my sunshine" that
the lady at the piano played in a style that made them all
sound like hymns   while a third woman a hefty but
    attractive middle aged lady turned them all into waltzes
    that she danced without rest

and we went in to watch and to
listen   and for the study in contrasts the different
   sweetnesses of them   the snowy haired lady at the organ
  providing a faint spiritual lift to all of the tunes a kind
of churchly resolution   while the singer   who had surely
 been an actress or an entertainer of some kind or another
    was performing them in the true twenties spooning style
and the dancer kept turning energetically and monotonously in
   always the same dance
              soon my mother-in-law who was seated with my mother
    and elly and me on a couch at the side of the room began
singing along   a trilling and birdlike obligato in her very
      sweet voice   while i sat beside her looking about the
  room and listening watching a dapper elderly gentleman
     flirting in a courtly way with a gray haired lady seated
next to him   and my mother-in-law stopped singing and said
 to me "you know this is a very nice place"   "yes" i said
"it is   with the party and the dancers and this music now
      it feels like maudes on cabaret night"   but she looked
 at me blankly and turned to the music again   and the
 pianist who had just finished "when the moon comes over the
mountain" abruptly launched into a rousing performance of the
   wedding march at which the singer threw up her hands and
 said "thats all for me   never again" and sat right down
next to us laughing and out of breath   and we talked for
  a while as the evening ran out and we took our leaves and
 went home

           the next day we got a telephone call about six
   o'clock in the evening   from my mother who usually calls
at that time because everybodys gone into supper and she can
  call from the desk and wont have to call collect   because
 its long distance from san diego to del mar and she can never
 find enough of her coins for a long distance call

            so she calls and says "hello david"
            and i say "hello mother"
            and she says "why dont you ever call me   i never
see you"
            "but mother" i say "i saw you yesterday"
            "oh" she says "i dont remember that"

　　　　i said ask jeanette　　she says "jeanette do you
remember seeing them yesterday"　　but jeanette doesnt
remember　　i said "mother　　tell me　　do you have anything
strange in your pocketbook　　a little box you dont
recognize"　　she said "i dont think so"　　i said "open your
purse and look"

　　　　she opens it up and says "yes theres a box in here
what is it?"

　　　　"its candy " i said

　　　　"candy　　what could i be doing with candy"

　　　　that may be a little less than adequate duration
even for me

90

during the talk i had taken the broomstick that was
on the stage and laid it across the two different size
stools making an awkward airplane seat   brought the formica
table up in front of the two stools to put my tape recorder
and notebook on and dragged over the blackboard   on which i
drew a soft edged rectangle to represent an airplane window
within whose frame i would from time to time bounce up to
draw and redraw schematic images of the landscape that i had
described as passing below us on the flight   this use of
props produced a somewhat unusual performance for me and i
was curious about its effect   at dinner i asked my art
historian friend if i was like the traditional storyteller
she said "no"

back in 1986 when i went up to san francisco to
give this talk at new langton arts   i was thinking about
who might be there in the audience   because i always like
my pieces to have some sense of direct address   i thought
that joel would probably be there and   as ellys cousin he
and i had had a long and close relation   so that i knew
he was still feeling the effects of the sudden breakup of
his second marriage   because the separations of men and
women always raise questions about who one has been living
with   and who one is   so i decided that in this piece
i wanted to think about the ground of the self   a subject
joel and i had been thinking about for a long time   though
in different ways   and because narrative lies at the core
of my ideas about the structure of the self   this piece is
filled with stories of people who were more closely related
to joel than many of the ideas   and as joel said to me
later "its not really criticism"

the price

when i thought about doing this piece i intended to
call it "where are you?"   because i wanted to think
through some ideas i had about the self   and because
thinking for me means asking questions   to which at the
start i dont have answers   and this title took the form of
a question addressed as much to myself as to you   and was
i suppose   something of an answer   or at least a
response   to a review of a talk i gave in new york the year
before   in which someone complained that i suffered from a
belief in the unitary self and had not enjoyed the benefit of
french deconstruction   which should have disabused me of
this illusion

now even i have felt the french breath of
deconstruction   unimpressed with it as i am   but i am
still interested in the self   though i never thought i
believed in its unity in so flatfooted a way as all that
i always thought the idea of the self was surrounded by
questions   and in fact what i was interested in were
precisely those questions   which were questions i spent a
lot of time asking   because i didnt know the answers   for
if i knew the answers i wouldnt have any reason to
ask the questions   and one of the questions im interested
in asking is   what is the locus of the source or ground
of the self   so when i thought of the title for this talk
as "where are you?"   what i had in mind was to look for the
place where the self   or what i take to be the self   has
its ground

now that self need not be so unitary as all that

it depends on what kind of ground it emerges from   how
it emerges from it   how continuously it emerges and how
uniformly it presents itself on emerging   and maybe it
doesnt really emerge   maybe it only hovers about a certain
place   this hovering a kind of complex act performed by a
number of actors whose interaction we could call the self

now that may sound more fragmentary or more like
teamwork   but what i was thinking was that this may be one
reason why in my pieces i can suddenly drop from a kind of
analytic or descriptive treatment into narrative

of course i
like narrative   i like stories as much as anyone else
but thats not the reason i tell them   it may be that
one of the things that makes it tolerable to me when i have
to do it is   that i want to do it and   like doing it   but
theres something else

it seems fairly evident to me that the
self could not exist without narrative

at one time i was very
interested in reading everything that anyone had to say about
narrative   i thought everybody would have said the
relevant things and i could find them out put them in my
pocket and not have to think about it any more

it turned out there was a great deal written about
narrative and much of it is very smart   but very little to
the point of what i wanted to think about   which was how
is it possible to imagine that you can continue to answer to
your name   whatever name that is   in a serious way   or
that you can maintain a continuous consciousness and have
a sense of its boundaries   unless its tested against
something that opposes and isnt it

in other words   we all go
by names   we know our names and we sit behind them and
answer to them in a way thats meaningful   we have a sense
of who we are and what we identify with and what we dont
and we wouldnt have this sense unless we had a series of
experiences that could convince us that we were the person
who had done this or failed to do that   or had wanted to do

94

this or had been afraid of doing that   and thinking about
it for a long time   ive come to believe that the reason i
use stories so much is that i think the self   however you
  may define it   is entirely constructed out of the
collision of the sense of identity with the issues of
narrative
              now this may seem purely theoretical but i'm not
interested in it in a purely theoretical way   yet i would
still like to distinguish in my own mind what i mean by
narrative
              i dont simply mean story   everybody generally
means story when they say narrative   but i would like to
distinguish between two things   one i would call narrative
and the other story   and as i see it theyre related   but
  not the same   story is a configuration of events or parts
of events that shape some transformation   but narrative
    or so it seems to me   is a sort of psychic function
  part of the human psychic economy and probably a human
universal   at least we identify it with being human   and
it involves a particular paradoxical confrontation

              consider the possibility of being confronted by a
  potential transformation   think of some thinking mind some
subject   some experiencing human being   even a very
  elementary one
                    at some point this being   encounters the
possibility the likelihood of transformation   this might be
  a disaster or it might be marvelous   but in any case
anything that undergoes transformation is not the same   and
there is always the threat that whatever it is that is
confronting transformation may not be preserved in it   and
  under the impact of that transformation may cease to be

              now my sense is that the center of narrative is
the confrontation of experience   an experiencing subject
with the possibility of transformation   the threat of
  transformation or the promise of transformation   these two
possibilities adjust it a little differently in terms of
  desire   and without desire there can be no narrative

but one of the fundamental things we desire   is
to continue to be
                              obviously there are occasions when we may
experience the desire not to be   but these are desperate
moments   more commonly we desire to be different   and
  what we really desire is that we will be the ones who will
be different   we want to be different but we want to be
  us   at least i know that if i want to be different i want
to be better but its me who i want to be better   i dont
  want to be so much better that i wont recognize in the me
who has become better the me that i used to be   and even
  more important   i want to be sure that the i who does the
recognizing is the same i who wanted to be better   or what
  sort of recognizing could it do and what would it mean to
be better

              at bottom nobody wants to become something totally
  other   if youre totally other youre cut off like an island
thats lost touch with the shore   so what if you become a
  prince a god or a king?   all fairy tales tell you stories
that have a certain lie at the center   that you want to
  become this other and that in becoming it theres no danger
  that you'll no longer be you   they know that its you the
pauper kid the little shlepp the   misshapen one who wants
to be the great powerful one   that you want to carry the
tiny inadequate awful one into the triumph   of being the
little one who's won out over the vicious dragon the terrible
  queen the horrible giant   crossed over the monstrous chasm
      and be on both sides of it
                              but you also know theres
something ridiculous about the idea of standing on both sides
  of a chasm   and wildly improbable   that makes the idea
  of the impending change more terrifying than the fearful
difficulties of achieving it   no matter how much you desire
  it   and its out of that clash that the self appears

            you may want to be different or you may want to be
  the same and something is coming at you   and something is
happening that makes you afraid that you may never be the
  same again   and you say i want my sameness to hold on all

96

the same   i want to survive
                              this lust for survival comes
from the confrontation with a transformation that will break
into your being and take you away from yourself   and if it
takes you away from you   theres nothing left of you to be
a self   nearly all cultural tragedy revolves around this
ground
                    the abraham and isaac story the iliad   abraham
leading his son up the hill to the sacrifice that would leave
him no longer a father   a transformation he never has to
undergo but has to contemplate to the point of terror   of
losing not only his only son but himself   in losing that
fundamental constituent of his selfhood his deeply desired
fatherhood
                    which is driven in upon him when isaac calls out to
him in the first quoted words of the ascent

                              "father?"

          that abrahams answer accepts and asserts as his identity

                              "here i am"

          while the iliad in its different and apparently
nonpsychological way takes three books of mythological
apparatus to bring priam to achilles' tent to beg back the
body of hector from his dead son's killer so he can provide
him with decent funeral rites   supplying all that narrative
time to contemplate the meaning of a confrontation   that
verges on the annihilation of the old king's royal and
paternal sense of self

                    or what it does is pose priam's royal and political
self and part of his paternal self
                                        achilles was the enemy of
his kingdom   slayer of his greatest son
                                        against his pious
paternal self   hector was dead and required decent burial
rites
          the way genesis poses abrahams sense of himself as jew
against his fatherhood
                              and out of these threatened

                                                            97

transformations   one that took place and one that didnt
     the selves of abraham and priam were defined   the
doctrinal self and the tragic self

          now its interesting that these two self defining
     confrontations of the jewish and hellenic traditions are
among the most celebrated narratives that our western culture
of relics has preserved   possibly because they incarnate
fundamental versions of a paradox on which the structure of
the self is based   this collision with an otherness
     that it might become and recognizes it is not   which
contains the beginning of a social construct that an original
unbounded consciousness does not
                                        the self has to be a
     localized consciousness with some sense of where it stops
     and it learns this against the wall of what it isnt and
might and might not become

          now in this sense every subjectivity is social to
     the extent that it is localized consciousness   but to
become a self it has to survive the collision or union with
other things and endure   it has to somehow rebound and
remain distinct   otherwise it is everything and nothing
     which is not a self or even a subjectivity   and
certainly not an agent   and if it is incapable not only of
actions but of distinguishing actions   or placing a value
on the outcome of events   this unlimited and indistinct
     consciousness is a delusive and socially useless system
     which only a romantic or religious sensibility can even
vaguely imagine   and then only as a condition contrary to
experience and to fact

          now if this is true and i am right   then what
narrative at its core celebrates or ritually reenacts is this
grounding of self   over the threat of its annihilation
     yet it still seems reasonable to ask if every story in
the world contains within it this threat of self annihilation
     and here is where my distinction between narrative and
story comes in
                         because i would hold that a story is merely

the configuration of events or parts of events that shape a
possible transformation   a temporal configuration of events
that marks the passage of one articulated state of affairs
into a significantly different one   which when it engages
the desires and fears of an experiencing subject represents
the external shell or surface manifestation of a possible
narrative   but it is the engagement with the possibility of
change that is the fundamental issue

                                    because any event that
is of any significance at all must change you   and the
degree to which it changes you is the degree to which it is
a threat to your existence   because change is not sameness
     as soon as youre aware of the danger of being different
     or the desirability of being different   it comes at a
price

               what price   what kind of price   what kind of
price do you want to pay for it   the first thing you think
of is people paying prices for things   heroic prices
     sometimes failing to pay prices for things defines
people   i can think of someone whose entire life was a
series of accommodations   who could think of his life as a
series of accommodations   like the vicar of bray

               i'm thinking of a famous russian journalist who
began his career on the side of the revolution before there
was a revolution   and found himself with doubts about it
when it came   but came to terms with it and everything else
that came to be in russia between 1917 and 1967   from
kerensky to brezhnev   and managed to thrive under the reds
and the whites   under lenin and stalin and khrushchev and
brezhnev   and survived every change in climate and power
while writing book after book hundreds of articles and a
     nearly unending succession of memoirs that reveal no great
     personal strain   and maybe finally no sense of person at
all
     now this man was a survivor   no matter what happened he
could always make do and as he trotted around the world as a
     soviet spokesman and journalist from france to germany to
spain and the balkans   attending writers congresses and

99

conferences   he made no mention of the executions of
bukharin and radek   and had little or nothing to say of the
suicides of friends like mayakovsky and tsvetaeva   or of
the imprisonment and murder of other friends and associates
like babel and meyerhold and mandelstam and feffer and
markish and bergelson   and under the circumstances of
russia and of survival perhaps he couldnt have been expected
to

        but if somewhere in this man's mind there was a
narrative   which couldnt appear in his writings   it
would have to have been based on his sense of self as a
survivor   his sense of what he had done or hadnt done
    or declined or neglected or refused or failed or been
unable to do   and what had happened as a consequence   or
in spite of or irrelevant of that   and what he felt about
the self that was the outcome of this history   this agent
or victim or witness who had managed to survive   at a price
    because every self holds itself together   to the
degree that it holds its self together   at a price
                                        which
need not be a heroic price
                            i know that what first comes to
mind for almost all of us is something like an image of
nathan hale his natural blonde hair tied back from his
handsome face in a simple knot hands tied behind his back
confronting his british captors   "i only regret that i
have but one life to give for my country"   but thats only
one kind of self
                        there is also a survivor self who doesnt
want to be nathan hale   who despises the nathan hales of
the world or is at least slightly contemptuous of them
because he considers them a little stupid or naive or
childishly idealist
                        this is a realist or cynical self who
separates himself from ideology and sentimentality who could
regard the political purges and pacts with the same mixture
of level headed regret and equanimity any other person might
reserve for traffic accidents and bad weather

this is obviously not an achilles self or priam
self   but think of it the shiftiness the shifting shape of
this self   that can fold itself around whatever comes
without tearing   the mensheviks the bolsheviks the
constitutionalists the bolsheviks again the leninists   and
in the end the stalinist imperium   a fair part of the
russian bureaucracy must have survived this way   as
functionaries   the way some functionaries of the weimar
republic must have survived under hitler and again under
the allies and into the government at bonn   and there are
functionaries in our government who have survived
changes from johnson to nixon to carter and reagan   because
for them politics is a government job and a mode of survival
and they know that the policies they implement are less
important and less likely to be realized than the forms they
follow which have the rocklike durability of custom and habit
and are sure to outlast the contingent and fragile ideas
that outsiders naively suppose that they serve

but even a nearly perfect functionary   because no
one is absolutely perfect   can sometimes be distracted from
his function by an ideal   not that he or she will be
derailed by it
if they are nearly perfect they will still
keep on track   but there will come even for them one or
two moments when they must consider a choice   an
alternative action   an alternative to being a functionary
because every functionary knows the story of nathan hale
and has an idea of what it might be like to look disdainfully
over the redcoat bayonets and say "i only regret that i have
only one life to give for my country"   even though they
may despise both hale and his country and say to themselves i
am not only not nathan hale but ive never wanted to be nathan
hale and i dont admire nathan hale   what i want is a quiet
life in the country or a condominium with a swimming pool and
a jacuzzi   and anyone who wants anything else is stupid or
a troublemaker

but the knowledge that thats what you want and how
much you want it and are willing to pay for it is also an

organization of a subjectivity around the fault line of some
   potential narrative crisis   that might dry up your jacuzzi
   or evict you from your condominium or force you to share it
with a family of lepers   which could change your life   so
   radically it might destroy your self   and destroy your
sense of self   so youve simply made a different choice
      but you know it

            now my wife's father   her real father not her
   poet and painter stepfather   was once faced with a
narrative situation that may throw a little light on this
      though it was not a matter of being nathan hale because
there was no possibility of it   it was the kind of
situation that could very commonly have been encountered by a
child living on the russian polish border around the time of
the first world war   because his little town was overrun
by the austrians and then by the russians and then the
   germans   who left it in control of the poles   who were
      driven out by the soviet russians   who finally retreated
and left them under control of the poles again   and each
of these armies set up its own form of government over the
   town   which was different from the last one   and as soon
as the people got used to one army they had to get used to
   the next

            now the jews of the town they didnt mind the
   austrians and the germans   because they could speak to
them   though they sympathized most with the soviets in
spite of the cossacks among them   and they uniformly hated
   the poles   who also hated them   but there were troubles
with all of them   because armies are always living at
least in part off the lands that they occupy   and no matter
how enlightened the army or how friendly the population
   there are always differences of opinion about the food and
   the fuel that the armies feel theyre requisitioning and the
people feel that they're stealing

            but the soviet commander was trotsky and he was
very sensitive to this   and he had given strict orders to
   shoot any soldier caught stealing from the people or

molesting their women   and orders are orders but soldiers
are soldiers and a drunken corporal had staggered out of a
bar with a bottle of vodka and decided he needed a herring
with it   so he commandeered a herring from the next door
shop   and the shopkeeper and some of his friends made a
complaint to the commanding officer and were surprised to see
the corporal arrested   and the whole town was even more
surprised to hear that the corporal had been convicted and
sentenced to death for taking a herring

       and then they were disturbed and a delegation of
elders and the shopkeeper and his cousin the coachman went to
the commanding officer to plead for clemency for the corporal
    but the commander said that bolsheviks were not thieves
and the corporal was a thief so that he was not a bolshevik
and therefore he was a traitor who would be shot in the
morning and he sent them away

       now my father-in-law was a little boy but he was
very talented in mathematics and it was decided that when he
was older he would go to the university at vilna so that he
had to go to the neighboring town to take lessons from a
math tutor every morning   and because it was a long walk
across the fields to the next town he had to start out very
early   and it was a walk he used to enjoy in the springtime
when the birds were out and drops of water were still
clinging to the spiderwebs and the grasstops though it got
his feet wet   and he was making his way past a clump of
trees at the edge of a field when he saw two soldiers at the
other side of the field watching another one digging   and
he went and hid behind a tree and continued to watch till
they took away his shovel and stood him in front of the hole
he was digging picked up their rifles and shot him

       thats the way my father-in-law tells the story
    and he tells it as a story   he doesnt tell it as
a narrative   he tells it as a story in which the full
confrontation is frozen and his own subjectivity is somewhat
frozen   its as if he comes to the brink of a narrative he
doesnt dare become part of   and for very good reason

because what could he have done and who could blame him?
he was just a little kid   could he have rushed up to the
executioners and said "oh don't kill him dont kill him kind
sirs please dont kill him for only a herring"   and would
they have listened?   so he ran and hid and who could have
blamed him   he was just a little kid the soldiers were far
away and he hardly knew what was happening

or thats the way he tells it and my father-in-law
has told us this story something like three times and he
always tells it the same way   so that im beginning to
think that there is something emblematic about this story
that has narrative aspects that he's always been thinking
of engaging and never engaged with   because whatever the
story starts out to illustrate   whether its the futility
of dealing with authorities or the bad outcome of good
intentions   there is always the memory of the helpless
child who didnt know what was happening yet knew enough to
hide and saw it happen   and was transformed into someone
who was then in some sense complicit with the scene

thats a harsh verdict and its not our verdict   we
know he wasnt really complicit with the scene   a nine or
ten year old kid   we know it wasnt his fault   but we
werent there in his head   watching him watching and the
feeling gradually growing that he knew more than he wanted to
be knowing   and because of that coming to feel he was a
part of that story even though he had no way of changing its
ending   so in my sense he felt complicit with the scene
because he watched it and didnt do anything   because
anyone who truly witnesses such a scene feels complicit with
the scene if he doesnt do anything   because part of being a
subject is the feeling that you can act

this may be an
illusion you may not be able to act   or you may only be
able to act at a price that may be much too great to pay
and nobody may expect you to pay it   and still you may
feel that somehow you should have done something because
your mind doesnt want to think of the price when it considers
the absolute alternatives to doing nothing and my sense is

that at the bottom of his story is the feeling "i shouldnt
   have seen such a thing"   not because they shouldnt have
   shown it to me   but because the seeing of it implies that
i have to do something   and i think that he tells this
story not so much out of a feeling of guilt
                                    not out of a
   feeling of guilt deeply engaged in his soul crying out "i
feel guilty   please forgive me for not doing anything"
      because he knows all the reasons as well and better than
we do   that he was too small too ineloquent   a little boy
   innocent and powerless who nobody would hold responsible for
doing nothing   except that in telling the story he comes up
   against his own experience of being there   and the same
sense that gave him the feeling of being there also gave him
   the feeling of being a part of that senseless killing from
   which he ran away   that carries with it a feeling of some
   kind of responsibility

         so whenever he tells that story he comes to the
   edge of a narrative in which he stands at the brink of a
terrible transformation   which if he chooses to experience
   could prove horrifying   and which he characteristically
   deflects with a laugh   but by repeatedly approaching and
resisting the transformation that entering this narrative
   would force on him   what he approaches in this story   at
least in its repeated tellings   is very much like narrative
   as i have defined it   but it is a narrative of the
   narrative situation   of the threat and terror of a
narrative which could if experienced transform my
father-in-law's self beyond his own recognition

         and yet at the same time if i am right   his
   continued resistance to this threat is a fundamental self
constituting act   that has no parallel that i can see in
   the life of ilya ehrenburg   or at least as far as i can
   tell from reading his memoirs   which give the impression
   that he simply walked away from the '36 trials or stalins
anti-jewish purges because that was all a reasonable man
   could do   because it is after all possible that he simply
   chose not to make his consciousness public   and ultimately

105

it is a matter of whether that consciousness perceives an
impending event as a threatening transformation that
determines whether or not we are dealing with narrative

so that a particular consciousness chooses its
narratives   though it may feel as though certain narratives
choose you   but they choose you by the   character of
your consciousness to begin with

which is to say that by the
grain of your consciousness your narratives are chosen   and
by what they do to your consciousness your self is formed

now i dont have any idea what causes the particular
grain of a consciousness   the particular angle of vision
that makes you tell those stories that way   the way my
mother   who was not much of a storyteller

in a family of
eloquent storytellers she was completely impoverished   in a
family that spoke a swarm of languages my mother spoke only
one   a fluent and articulate pennsylvania english that she
learned after coming to this country at about seven or eight
and the others that she understood but apparently
rejected   spoke poorly and ineptly   and as a consequence
cut herself off from a vast reservoir of memories and
capabilities   so that she remembered very little of her
childhood or at least very seldom reminisced about it and only
ever told one story that i remember hearing

she was a very little girl and her grandmother was
ill and this was in southern russia somewhere outside odessa
and my mothers grandfather was a very wealthy man with a
large estate who supported a large number of his married
children in a patriarchal manner   and my mother's mother my
grandmother was aware that her mother-in-law was ill and
sent my mother   who was then a very little girl of perhaps
four or five to stay with her grandmother   and this sounds
very primitive   to sleep with her and keep her warm   as
my mother told it

and the little girl   my mother remembers
being frightened of my grandfather's estate with its big dogs

106

and cows and horses   and of her grandmother who had a
mustache and snored and was unpleasant and cold   and she
felt very alone in this huge house with her giant grandfather
and his servants in the giant rooms   and she woke up or
half woke up in the middle of the night and was very
frightened in the dark   and in her half sleep got out of
bed and wandered from room to room looking for her mother
    and feeling her warmth   stretched out her arms to
embrace her and climb into bed beside her   and instead of
her mother embraced a stove and was horribly burned

        this may be the only story my mother ever told
    and i suppose it was an emblematic story for her   and
while i'm not exactly sure where the narrative is   i
suspect it is retrospectively situated in the mind of the
narrator spectator   who sees the impending danger of
reaching out for warmth and love and watches in growing
horror as the child holds out her arms to the stove   but as
a story it is a gruesome cautionary tale with a moral   "if
you reach out for anything you will surely get burned"
    that i think must have been self defining   because of
its similarity to another story that my mother never told
but had a persistent attachment to

        it was not a personal story and i would never have
known of her attachment to it except for my curiosity about
her reading   my mother was fairly literate   she had a
high school education and i think a little bit of college
when that kind of education was not so common   and when
she was younger she'd had a fairly large collection of novels
    like *point counterpoint* and *the sound and the fury* that she
must have read some time and kept in her bedroom for years
till they disappeared in a move from one apartment to another
and she always read and liked to read   but in her later
years she seemed to have fixed on books with biblical
subjects   which i thought was kind of strange since she'd
never been religious
                    most of these books were novels about
the history of the jews or about the jewish background of
jesus and i imagined they were a little bit like some of the

movies of her childhood or cecil b. de mille spectaculars and
   i didnt think too much about them   but there was one book
that she had about which i got fairly curious

            even when i still lived in new york i didnt see her
   very often   maybe once every few weeks   but whenever i
saw her she seemed to be reading one particular book that was
sitting on top of her night table   and as far as i could
   tell she'd been reading this book for a couple of years
      and i asked her about it because it was a higher
theological analysis of the bible edited by some group of
scholars i think from the union theological seminary   and i
wondered what could have attracted her to this enlightened
   historical account of her biblical spectaculars and why she
had been reading it for over two years   and she told me she
   was reading it because she was interested in the meaning of
   the bible and it was very interesting but she was bothered
   by it because something she was looking for was missing

            and i said "well whats missing?" and i wondered
   what she meant   because anything could be missing   and
in a certain sense in a book like that everything could be
   missing   because in a higher theological account of the
bible whats present?   but i knew that she meant she had
   been looking for some particular thing that wasnt covered
by this scholarly account   and she said "i cant find
   anything about the tower of babel"

            at first i thought this was funny but slowly i
   realized that the tower of babel is another emblematic story
for her   another cautionary tale with the same or nearly
   the same moral as the story of the burned child because my
   mother has always had a dire image of the consequences of
aspiration   any kind of aspiration and these architects
   were wise guys who thought they were going to get to heaven
   by means of skill and intelligence and education   and
   they were destroyed for their arrogant presumption   thats
what did it to them and the result of all their efforts
and skill and education was that their building was destroyed
   and they were left all alone

now she never told me this but i can infer it from
the rest of her life   my mother was a professional widow
     she was one of those women who if you asked them what
are you would say im a widow   she became one after my
father died   took a brief and difficult vacation from her
widowhood when she remarried twelve years later but returned
to it when she left her husband and was finally confirmed in
it when he died a few years later   and since she was a
professional widow she took a kind of pride in what she
regarded as her helpless and pathetic state   which i always
found very irritating because she tried to extend it to me
as a "fatherless child"

          so i usually paid very little attention to her
     but i will never forget that when i was going to high
school   which was an engineering high school   my mother
thought i was making a big mistake   she never understood
why i wanted to go to an engineering school
                                        which was because
i wanted to be an inventor
                              but i could never tell her that
     so i told her it was because i wanted to be an engineer
     and she said that wasnt a good idea   and i said why
not what should i be and she said a farmer
                                        there we were
living in brooklyn and i was the kind of kid who built
motors and radios and i had never seen a farm in my life and
i didnt want to   but i said what kind of farmer   and she
said a chicken farmer   she said we could go out to lakewood
and raise chickens   and the only chickens i had ever seen
were in pet stores at easter time or in butcher shops   it
was amazing to me then   but when she told me that what she
was looking for in her higher theological commentary was
the tower of babel i remembered her idea of chicken farming
and i realized it was the alternative to erecting a great
tower   because chicken farming was closer to the earth
     she probably should have said a potato farmer because
potatoes are even closer to the earth than chickens   but
     the only farming she knew about was out around lakewood

new jersey   where her more affluent relatives used to take
a two week winter vacation and bring us back taffy and
turtles from atlantic city   and most of the farmers around
lakewood raised chickens   but the basic idea was of being
  close to the earth and seemed based on the only yiddish
proverb she seemed to know

                              "dont raise me up to the heavens
  and i wont fall down to the ground"

                                          and it was as though she
  had a view of the hubris of all aspiration all reaching out
for achievement for love   she had done it once and gotten
  burned   or considering her widowhood had done it twice and
  look what had happened to her   and she had even tried
again   how many times can you take a chance on living?

        so in a certain sense my mother may have confronted
narrative in these two stories of reaching out for her mother
  and in the tower of babel   as the spectator trying to will
away a transformation that will exact a terrible price
        though in both cases the narrative center is located in
  the experience of a kind of narrator listener who watches
the story unfolding as she tells it and hears it and feels
  herself confronting the danger of being transformed

          now this act of confrontation is almost entirely
  absent   from the accounts of narrative given by the
structuralist thinkers like propp or bremond or lévi-strauss
    or todorov or roland barthes   because they are
  fundamentally externalists concerned with the articulation
  of story as a kind of abstract and generalized social
  production   and while they sometimes illuminate elegant
symmetries in the shapes of plots i dont think they are
  really relevant to a study of narrative at all   mainly
because they begin from texts instead of tellings   and
even if they come out of tellings they come out of more or
  less ritualized occasions that tend to obliterate the
narrative centers that arise from human social experience
        but stories that arise from ordinary social occasions
are always narrative   because they arise out of a
  circumstance in which you are talking and trying and

failing to make some kind of sense

      and the stories that they have collected are
usually nobody's telling and often a kind of synthesis of
  several people's tellings   or else they treat them as
nobody's telling   where nobody is trying to make any
particular sense   and this has been a large part of the
  folklorist tradition and is certainly true of the
collection of the grimms and of afanasiev   and when a
story is nobody's telling the narrative starts to go out of
  it and appears only as a possibility or a set of
possibilities   and if the organization of the story was
originally the outcome of someone struggling to make some
  sense out of a narrative crisis   then a study of these
story collections is a study of monsters like thalidomide
babies and provides almost as much misinformation as
information about the structure of narrative   so that what
  you need to bring to this teratology   to make any sense
out of it is a lot more understanding of the kind of
story that emerges directly from discourse   where there is
  always a narrative stake
                    and what im thinking of by way of
example is not even a story yet   it will only become one if
  i tell it
      my mother-in-law was a very gutsy and bold
businesswoman who made a career out of running resort hotels
  for which she never had adequate resources   but she was a
woman of wonderful beauty and charm and gaiety with which
she imbued her nearly always bankrupt hotels that she almost
  always managed to get people to back   always inadequately
and year after year   and she had creditors and mortgages
and trust deeds and charming buildings on beautiful grounds
in the mountains   and she balanced them all with the skill
  of a juggler to remain the impresario of a great enterprise
that never rewarded her sufficiently for the energy she put
into it   though that never mattered because the way she saw
  herself was as the impresario of a high class resort in the
mountains   but finally her energy ran out   and then her
  luck ran out and she lost her last hotel

                                    but that wasnt all
        she began to lose track of the past   at first in
little pieces   and then in slightly larger ones   not the
very distant past   her life back in poland with her mother
        but pieces of the immediate past   like whether she had
salted the roast or what time she was supposed to meet
someone for lunch or where she had left her glasses or her
keys   and in the beginning this caused only small
difficulties
                    but she began to quarrel with friends for not
arriving on time   she began to believe that her husband
peter was hiding her keys and her glasses to humiliate her
and he began to be afraid that she would turn on the gas and
forget to light the oven or put weird things in the food
        and she began to feel so angry and restless that she
decided to take a trip back to new york to visit old friends
        but the trip was a disaster   she nearly blew up her
friend's kitchen she got lost in the streets and when she
came back to san diego and we picked her up at the airport
she had no idea what city she was in   though she had a
vague notion it was los angeles

        from there things went downhill fast   peter had
to spend more and more time with her because she was so
restless and he couldnt do any painting   so he nagged at her
telling her to write notes to herself and reminding her
constantly of whatever she forgot   and she got so furious
that she attacked him with a knife and stabbed him in the leg

        so we had to separate them then   and after a lot
of looking we found a residential hotel in east san diego
        collwood villa a home for active elderlies they called
it   and some of them were pretty active and took part in
all the activities the folkdancing and group sings and bible
lessons and attended the films on the fauna and flora of
new zealand and the lectures on the christian life or the
problems of ethiopia that scotty the social director arranged
for them   and some even had their own cars and went out
shopping   but most of them just sat around in the music
room or in the lobby or on the porches quietly talking to

each other or to themselves   or just sitting in company
waiting for dinnertime or lunch   and this was an
environment into which jeanette fitted just fine

    she went to all the folkdancing classes and
attended all the lectures and looked at all the films   and
if she forgot how to do steps or what the lectures were about
most of the others did too   and there was nobody to remind
her that she forgot   and she was quite happy in her
beautiful room with its persian rugs and plants and peters
lovely paintings on the walls   which she continued to take
pleasure in   although she'd forgotten completely about
peter whom she'd watched painting them and with whom she'd
    debated almost every color and form as she arranged for his
one man shows in new york city and then in san diego   but
i know she still took pleasure in them because when i once
mentioned how beautiful they were   she looked at them
intently for a while and with an airy medician gesture said
    "yes   i had them painted for me"
                                      so she was fairly
happy there though a little bit lonely and sometimes when we
came to see her we would find her pacing quickly up and down
the lobby with a slightly desperate look   though more often
we would find her sitting with several other ladies smiling
    or dozing while they chattered or kept silent   but after
a while we began to find her sitting with a gentleman   a
big hearty looking man with a great head of white hair and an
    easy way with the ladies   and he was always making jokes
and flirting with all of them   with etta the manager and
scotty the social director   and with all of the active
    elderly ladies who still had it together enough to know he
was flirting

        and more and more we would find jeanette hanging
around with harry when we came to visit   and as he got to
know us he would give us a big greeting   he would hold out
his hand and say "hiya sport" to me and "hello beautiful" to
ellie   "your mother's here take care of her now"   and he
would tactfully wander off to play cards for a bit   but
after a while they were always together and everybody began

to recognize them as a couple   even the people who ran the
place
        "the lovebirds they call them   theyre inseparable"
scotty said   "i think theyre even sleeping together though
  you know its against the rules"

            so whenever we came to visit we took harry with us
  up to jeanette's beautiful room surrounded by the paintings and
  the persian rugs and the plants that were mostly dead now
  because jeanette couldn't remember to water them   and we
  talked as well as we could given jeanette's fading memory
      but harry made lots of good humored bad jokes and we
  found out that his family had come from rumania to the lower
  east side   where he realized he liked girls better than
  school   so he became a tailor and had a family   and
  somehow he'd come out to san diego where he'd also had a
  tailor shop   although he'd left the rest of his family
  somewhere back in the east
                            or we sort of found this out
  because harry though he was very direct and hearty when he
  spoke was always a little vague about details   and if you
  interrupted any of his rambling stories with questions he
  would get confused and stop and start somewhere else   and
  even if he looked more capable than jeanette there were
  limits to his capabilities   he was always losing his
  glasses and to make up for this he was always picking up
  everybody else's   any time anybody put down a pair of
  glasses near harry he picked them up and put them in his
  breast pocket   so whenever any of the management people
  were looking for anyone's glasses they would check out all of
  harry's pockets   and he would always deny having them and
  when they found them he would protest they were his   to
  prove it he would put them on and then look a little bit sad
  and sheepish when they turned out to be an impossible fit

            and he was always losing his clothes   sweaters
  and shirts and slacks some of which would wind up in the
  drawers of jeanette's bureau   and elly would try to hide
  them for him in jeanette's closet   because once they escaped
  from jeanette's room they were gone forever   and after a

while he had so few clothes he took to wearing one of
jeanettes sweaters   which since she was barely five feet
tall and he was over six looked a little ridiculous   so we
bought him a cardigan and told him it was for christmas
but all things considered their lives were going well
jeanette had forgotten her first husband she had
forgotten peter her painter husband and was now living
contentedly with harry   and then they changed the
management

residential hotels for active elderlies are
business propositions and are usually part of some financial
management portfolio   usually with other kinds of real
estate investments like shopping centers or office buildings
and when one management company for tax advantages or
for cash flow trades one of these hotels to another
management company for an interest in a shopping mall or an
industrial park the lives of the residents usually change
sometimes for the better sometimes for the worse   this
was no exception

the company managing collwood villa was fairly
remote and its daily life was managed more or less
effectively by etta   a tough but good natured hulk of a
woman with a staff of pallid underpaid and overworked
middle-aged ladies who dispensed medications planned the
meals looked after the clothing answered the telephones and
generally supervised the fading lives of the residents
while etta watched over the crew of equally underpaid latino
cleaning ladies and maintenance men who kept the place from
falling apart   and scotty the social director supplied the
spiritual needs
as managers went etta ran a fairly loose
ship   people usually got their medications on time got to
their dental appointments had their clothes cleaned and lived
on reasonable institutional food   but one day we came to
visit and etta was gone   and so were all the middle-aged
ladies   replaced by kids
of the old staff only scotty was
left looking nervous and only a shadow of her usually

theatrical self   and in the office was a heavily made-up
platinum blonde with false eyelashes and pink fingernails
 that we got to call dragon lady
                              the dragon lady ran a tight
ship   the people either got their medications on time or
not   got to their doctor's appointments more or less on
time and ate pretty much the same food   but dragon lady
was big on regulations for her tenants   "they must not be
in each other's rooms" scotty said   "it's strictly against
the rules"
            it had been against the rules in etta's time too
but nobody much cared and we were on the point of asking
etta to get them a bigger bed because harry was so big   now
we were given to understand that dragon lady cared   and
ellie tried to explain that harry forgets he gets confused
    i'm sure he thinks he's in his own room   but scotty
insisted things would have to change
                              "she's a stickler for
rules"

            she instituted lots of them   about clothing about
meals   she made a new rule that everybody had to be done
with breakfast by 8:30 or would not be fed   now harry was
used to sleeping late and charming the kitchen help into
giving him a sweet roll and a cup of coffee when he came down
at nearly ten   dragon lady was not susceptible to charm
 and she wouldnt allow her staff to be   so they refused
harry his morning coffee   we got a call from scotty
    "jeanette is acting up and you'll have to put a stop to
 it"

            what had happened was that when the staff refused
to serve harry his coffee the old jeanette who used to
manage huge hotel staffs charming and bullying crazy chefs
drunken dishwashers and sinister handymen reemerged   and
she made a glorious scene   "in my hotel" she told them "a
man always has a right to his coffee   you will serve him
now or you're fired"   it was a marvelous flareup   but she
wasnt in her hotel she was in collwood villa home of active

elderlies and we were afraid they might throw her out   so
we had to come down and cool it   and elly had to suggest
to harry that he would be better off if he got up a little
earlier   though she knew he would never remember to

so we brought them an electric alarm clock and set
it for seven and i tried to work on dragon lady who for some
reason seemed to like me   and i suggested patience and
tolerance   that the rules were new and would take getting
used to but that things would work out i was sure   and she
was sure too   but as we were going out scotty reminded us
once more about the sleeping over
"it must not go on we've got rules"
"even for lovebirds scotty?" i said
"even for lovebirds" she said and looked away

we knew this was only the beginning of trouble
harry wasnt good at rules   there were too many of them
it was like being in school and harry was never good at
school   he found school unpleasant and found it more
pleasant to fit people's clothing   and he left school at a
time when nobody cared and made a living as a tailor   and
he was doing very well and he lived a pleasant life without
school and he didnt feel that he had to take any orders he
didnt like   and here were all these young people giving him
orders and threatening to take away his privileges if he
didnt follow their orders   and he didnt know what
privileges they meant but he didnt like their orders or
intend to take them and he was furious with them   so we
knew it was not going to work out

and one day we came down there and harry was gone
jeanette was pacing up and down the hallways looking
desperately alone and scotty explained "it was unacceptable
behavior   there was nothing else to be done"   harry had
been in a rage and fought back   and his fight took the
form of pissing on them   he pissed on their potted palms on
their rubber plants on their philodendrons and on their
begonias   and when they first caught him peeing on their
plants they thought he was confused and they took him to the

117

bathroom   but it happened again and again   one day the
dragon lady was waiting for the elevator and when it opened
there was harry peeing into the corner   so he was gone

          we found out that they had sent him to an old age
home in la mesa   we were not his relatives and we didnt
know if there was anything we could do about it   but we
felt terrible looking at the black distracted look on
jeanettes face   and we went out to visit him   the place
was a ramshackle old stucco building at the end of a road
past some dismal small houses that looked like they were
waiting to be wrecked near a field of chaparral that had been
gutted by fire   it was a miserable little building with no
grounds but it was surrounded by a chain link fence

          we pulled into the driveway and went to look for the
central lobby where the old people would be sitting around
   socializing   and there was no central lobby for them to
sit around in   only a small space around a reception desk
where a clerk gave us harrys room number and pointed down a
narrow corridor where a few dazed people were aimlessly
walking up and down and a woman was standing in a doorway
   quietly weeping   and as we made our way down the corridor
the people in the rooms looked sicker and sicker   till we
got to his room

          we knocked at the door and there was harry sitting
in a chair next to his bed staring out of the window at the
charred sagebrush in the lot across the way   and he looked
at us   he got up   and he said "hiya big shot"   and
he gave me his hand   and he looked at ellie and he said
"hello beautiful"   and he sounded just like his old self

          so we spoke with him for a while   and we said
harry how do you like it here   and   he looked out at the
chaparral
                    "it's all right" he said
                    and we said "do you miss the old place?"
   because we thought if he really cared   even if we
werent his relatives   we'd put up a fight for him
                    "i'm here now" he said

we said "harry this place doesnt seem to
have the same kind of people   there's no lobby and the
dining room doesnt look so good   do you like it here?"
and he thought for a while and he looked at
us and he said
"the price is right"

and i dont think it was money he was talking about

dan peck asked me if i could do a talk piece at vassar
that could serve as a contribution to a volume that several
ex-students of sherman paul were preparing to honor his work
as a critic and scholar and teacher as he was nearing
retirement
and i liked the idea of doing a piece for sherman
who had written so generously and well of so many
contemporary poets   myself included and i had intimations
that he was feeling a little unnerved as anyone might who
was vigorous and strong and at the height of his powers
who was approaching the chronological age at which educational
instititions they had served and brought honor to bid them to
step out or down

at the same time i knew this was not so serious for
someone like sherman   whose life was not really an
institutional life   but a life of thought and work that he
would continue in the same way he had always proceeded only
with a bit more time for work on his house or his book or
whatever he felt like doing

still it would be a change and i thought i could
talk about change and the feeling about change because i had
recently been thinking about a change
i'd just had the
possibility of a change thrust at me with enough energy so
that i had to consider it   an east coast university had
made an inviting gesture toward me   and while i had no
need of a job   i was comfortable in my old one and maybe
for that reason i felt i had to consider whether i wanted to
consider it

and i did   however lightly

i came back from a skiing trip with a banged-up
knee and flew east to have a couple of conversations with
several intelligent and agreeable people in a wealthy and
dismal school in the great grey city of my childhood and i
felt depressed   and i had no reason to feel depressed or
no reasonable reason
                    i had no intention of taking their job
and they had no intention of giving it to me   they were
reasonable people in a distinguished institution that had
no interest in changing their impoverished departments of art
and were merely going through the motions of thinking they
were thinking about it   and they had invited me there only
to imagine an extreme possibility in their search for what
was probably an ordinary fundraiser   and i was there
merely to enjoy a free trip to the city and limp around
taking dozens of photographs of its once great and now
ruined park and get a look at some of the theater and art
that are the overestimated and only advantages that this
dying city offers to people like me   so i was doing what
i wanted to do   but i was depressed

i felt sad for the city of my childhood and its
ruined state   as i always feel sad for it as i see it every
year losing bit by bit of its neighborhoods its ukrainian
polish and czech neighborhoods   as it has already lost
its jewish neighborhoods and would eventually lose its
italian and spanish and even black ones   and was already
losing its artists to a remorseless real estate inflation
that had filled their places with a rich and bland expense
account world of stockbrokers and bankers and art directors
and advertising executives and the officers of multinational
corporations

but they were not serious and i was not serious
and it was as if only for that reason i had to consider
the purely virtual change in my life that this condition
contrary to fact would have subjected me to   and the idea
of coming back to the city of my childhood and youth as a
stranger   because i knew that it was no longer my city and

121

i used to think of it as my city   and now it was their city
and i had no use for them or their city and thats why i
felt sad as i rode down in the train from providence
*   where i also had something to do   to new york and then*
back up to poughkeepsie watching the spring trying to restore
some life to the ravaged eastern landscape while the search
committee was still deliberating

*   and the horror of the new beginning that i would*
never have to make pressed itself upon me with a weight
completely independent of its fictional character and i
realized i had something to say to sherman

the river

coming into a space like this   obviously a very
friendly space in that it has a very warm tone to it   in a
   way thats almost disconcerting for a poet   mainly because
what youre used to is the randomness of the road   the
   notion that youre going somewhere and you dont know where
that is or what its like   and youre going to go do your
talking poem   talk poem   talk piece   do your piece of
talking   which is a piece of talking   because essentially
   your talking is an ongoing enterprise   at least my
talking is   an ongoing enterprise that i try to relate to
   thinking
            because talking for me   is the closest i can come
      as a poet   to thinking   and i had wanted for a long
time a kind of poetry of thinking   not a poetry of thought
   but a poetry of thinking   since getting so close to the
process of thinking was what i thought the poem was   and
theres a sense i have that makes this kind of curious   a
   problematic enterprise   because in one sense when i talk
about what it means to go do talk poems ive used a
conversational model to explain what i meant

            this is a kind of dialogical model   that you go
   to places and imagine poetry as some kind of ongoing
discourse with people   but of course you dont know the
people youre going to talk to in any real sense
                                    you might get
   to know them later or you may imagine who they are but you
dont really know them   so its a kind of fantasy for me to
believe that every time i come into a place that i'm going to
   tailor a work   specifically for the properties or

necessities of some place that i really have no very powerful
grip on
          obviously i have to rely on the fact that i have
things on my mind before i get here   like most of you
     we poets   have an agenda a list of things we think
about   and i can only hope that the things i think about
    have something in common with the things you have on your
lists   though they may not form a perfect overlap   if
  they formed a perfect overlap there would be no need for me
to talk about them   and if they formed no overlap at all
     there would be no way i could talk about them   so the
imperfect fit is probably the ideal situation and thats a
good thing   because i have to face it anyhow
          and here we are   and being here ive been thinking
about doing yet another piece
                            and i do them with some
regularity
          not the regularity of the calendar
                                 i do them several
times a year   anywhere from five to thirteen times a year
i may do talk pieces   more than that gets to be a nuisance
and less than that i feel rusty   and this makes a
difference because i will also sit down and write   usually
  i will write only on the basis of pieces that i go out into
the world to do   usually i'll record them thats why the
tape recorder   i wont work on any one of them in advance
    but often i will go out and do one and take it back and
decide whether i want to make a version of that one in print
    and of course it sometimes changes as it goes onto paper
  because whatever winds up on paper is never exactly like
whats in the air   although what i want to do is bring an
image of talking out of the air and onto the page   to make
the claim of speech to make the claim of thinking   within
  the frame of the book
                       that im afraid i sometimes strain
significantly   and i want to make the claim for speech and
the claim for thinking in an environment in which i think the
claims for thinking have become somewhat rigid   and where
speech has no place into which it fits nicely   because
if you go into a library   and a library is the central

124

place in the institution of writing   there is no
  bibliographical category into which speaking fits   and if
  you go into a library and try to look it up you might not be
  able to find it   ive often thought how funny it would be
to look myself up in the library   but i suppose its no
funnier than looking up john cage   who either winds up in
music   which is not so reasonable as all that
                                                    sometimes it
may be reasonable but not for a book like *silence*   *silence*
    it seems to me should have wound up in the poetry
section of the library but it never does   it could have
wound up in the philosophy section and it doesnt   it
invariably winds up in the music section   and my books
    when i go out and look for them
                                            i dont often go out to
look for them   but because theres a streak of perversity
in me sometimes i do   i go to see if theyre in criticism
    theyre not   theyre not in prose   theyre not in the
fiction section   though they could be   because my
stories are not invariably true   or not altogether true
    i dont guarantee that   or at least theyre not always
fact
    and i look for my books and i dont know where they
should be anyway   because talking has no place in a library
            in fact i have a publishing problem with publishers
i used to have difficulty convincing new directions that they
    shouldnt list me in the poetry section   i never could
convince them   but i tried to convince them to put me in
    the prose section as well   and they didnt believe this
so they consistently placed me beside all the poets   many
of whom are my friends   but then people pick up my book
    expecting to find some kind of verse in it and they dont
find it   and not finding verse in it theyre afraid they
havent found poetry   which is not so much of a problem for
    me   but it is for a publisher if he starts to get returns
because of this
                    somebody says "this is not poetry take it
    back"   it doesnt usually happen like this   a book buyer
usually suffers for a bit and then sells the cause of his
    suffering to a second hand bookshop with maybe a couple of

nasty comments scribbled in the margins i suspect   but
thats all right   it makes a lively ongoing career for my
book

            but if i return to this issue of coming to a place
with things on my mind   one of the things thats often on
my mind is the question of beginning   but it seems
somewhat bizarre to put the question of beginning at the
    beginning of a piece   its something you should do later
because if you start with the question of beginning you say
do i begin here
                        what do i do take off my pack and unpack it
    come on in   dont worry   feel comfortable here sit
down i'm not easily interruptible and i dont worry
latecomers or interruptions   i once did a piece   a
performance at u.c. davis years ago   and they scheduled it
    in the cafeteria at lunch time   i guess poetry or my
poetry was not very popular there   and they were hoping to
get me an audience   and it was very funny   there was a
    lunch counter and a large crowd of students at tables   and
at one end was a little platform about eight feet around and
    two feet high   and while everybody was sitting and eating
and looking politely i was up on the platform doing my piece
    i would talk for a while   while walking around and
looking at someone i thought i was addressing because he was
eating his egg salad somewhat meditatively   and he would
    suddenly get up and leave   so i wasnt sure who i was
talking to and who was eating lunch   and whether there was
maybe some overlap between the two   when at one point a
very little kid who was there i guess with a lunching or
    listening mother or father   climbed up onto my two foot
high stage   and finding herself somewhat surprised to be
there while i was talking   began to wander around looking
for a way down

            and while i was talking i was suddenly afraid that
this tiny kid was going to walk to the edge and fall to her
    death   she was so very small   and while i was talking
she was getting nearer and nearer the precipice   and i
realized it was getting perilous   she was standing at the
    edge looking interestedly down   so i picked her up while i

126

was talking and offered her to the audience   and somebody
who had been sitting there rose up took the kid and sat down
to continue listening or eating   so it doesnt really
matter   if that didnt get me nothing else will

but once again this question of beginnings
because every time you start something its easy to give
the impression that youre really beginning   you can create
a kind of dramatic frame to suggest that some vast silence
had intervened for ages and now youre going to do the new
thing   you set it up and the lights dim   or else they
come up   you create an imaginary drum roll and you settle
in and you say   NOW   and of course theres something
preposterous about this something silly   because what
youve been doing has been going on all the time

ive been here much of the day   i arrived by train
which is very good because that lets you not feel the
kind of separation anxieties airplanes produce   i dont
even know if you can get here by plane   the hudson is not
an area you normally travel on a plane   but the thing
about a train is that youre never completely out of the space
you were in before   because the back of the train is still
in the same space that you were just in while the front of
the train is going into a space youre not in yet   so you
keep watching the hudson slide by you   looking at the
deteriorated landscape of new york as it depopulates itself
and its industry slips into the water   and you watch the
history of this countryside that i know fairly well because
i grew up here

i'm a new yorker as my accent will tell you
not only did i grow up in new york i also know its
countryside because at various times ive lived in upstate
new york   and i was interested to go through the
countryside again   watching the coming on of the spring
which is the kind of recurrent thing that makes you feel
youre always the same when youre not   its part of the
falsification system of nature   the recurrence of seasons
offers a false security that lets you think nothing has
changed   because the flowers come out on the trees   you
see the shadblow   you see the maples beginning to flower

and you think that because everything is going on its
going to continue going on and you dont think that youre
dying   you dont think that anything will really be born or
die
    though it looks like things are being born   because the
trees repeat their same boring performance year in and year
out to our immense delight   because its all very pretty and
delightful to look at   and you keep feeling reassured

        i felt like that when i was in new york city this
    morning and i felt like it all the time i was coming out
of new york city   and then i felt i was in the familiar
    hudson valley all the time   the familiar hudson valley
and i know its not familiar   because i know all the things
that used to be here   iron works disappear   mills and ice
    companies and tile factories and machine shops   you see
them disappearing

            coming up here one of the most amazing things was
looking at that toy-like castle   you must know it   its a
    kind of toy castle   a ruined toy castle that looked as
though some child had been playing soldiers   some oversized
kid playing with tin soldiers in a fit of rage reached out
with one hand and knocked over one and a half walls
    leaving this little island without its toy soldiers any
    more   it strengthened a feeling that had been building in
    me since i had come to the city a couple of days before
    where i had passed a day and a night with my brother-
in-law and sister-in-law
                        which is odd   why should i think of
    that   i suppose because i was coming from their apartment
    i was staying with them in a sunny apartment overlooking
new yorks central park   and central park is beginning to
    flower right now   and central park flowering   when it
happens once a year is kind of wonderful   it gives you an
    image of such seductive falseness   as it presents itself
and the city in an impossibly favorable light out of the past
    because it is suddenly an impressionist city   as
everything goes soft and golden green and slightly out of
focus   the leaves on the trees are too small to be seen as
leaves the colors are fainter the bushes are flowering

    128

forsythia and japanese cherry   and when the maples flower
its for a very short period a precarious moment   and it
convinces you that youre really looking at 1871   which you
still dont believe   because you know its not 1871 its the
spring of 1987   and you know that parts of the lake are
filled with garbage and the great terrace is ruined and the
ramble choked with weeds   but this grand english landscape
that never was in central park is still there at this moment

and from up where my brother-in-law and sister-
in-law live you can see almost the entire park   which is an
accident because theyre about to leave   theyve been living
there a while and now theyre going somewhere else   and
walking the floor of the light flooded apartment   in the
filtered spring sunlight falling on the floor youre standing
on   which came from idaho   its a golden schist that they
had rather startlingly shipped in from idaho   because it
was beautiful   at great effort   because the idaho schist
is different from the manhattan schist that underlies the
whole island   its more golden   it looks as though it has
pyrites in it
schist is that peculiar kind of metamorphic
rock that has granitic materials in it   but instead of
having a quartzlike hardness its flaky   and the manhattan
version has bits of mica glittering in it   and its
glamorous and kind of crappy at the same time   and new york
sits on this glamorous crappy metamorphic rock   over which
the soil seems to creep in a thin layer from under which
this grey rock crops out as if to let you know   that the
soil isnt very deep and that central park is not fertile meadow
it was a kind of swampy barren out of which olmsted and
vaux created their illusion of england so that the industrial
poor could learn to be citizens of a free republic

which was an astonishing idea but they had it or at
least olmsted had it   they built this park three miles
north of the city or two and a half miles north of it   so
that the throttled overworked and dangerous poor   who
choked the city and provided its economic base could come to
find a green place that was closer than the long trip to the
country of staten island   or the estates and farms of the

bronx   where it would be possible to enjoy the humanly
cultivated charms and fresh air and relative solitude of a
    nature otherwise unavailable to the working poor

                                                and theres
something in this   obviously the working poor were under
great pressures in the city   the long hours the low pay the
    miserable tenements and   the filthy streets   and in a
way i suppose that olmsted in 1858   looking at this city
was making a kind of promise to the city in his proposal
    he and vaux   because they did it together

                                            i know that
weve gotten into the habit of talking about olmsted as if he
were a single artist   and as far as the park venture went
    both central park and prospect park   it was a joint
venture

            calvert vaux the architect designer and frederick law
olmsted farmer and writer and practical administrator   that
    put the park together when the city knew that it had to do
something   because people had to be able to live together
    under conditions that were already hardly tolerable

    because the working people were already horribly crowded
together down at the southern end of manhattan island the
southern end that was already hardly habitable   since the
city had destroyed the greens around the battery and most of
the other small places where people could gather together in
a leisurely way outside of the saloons that every christian
    feared were the plague of the poor   and it had paved over
the little streams and the canal from which canal street
had gotten its name

            it had buried the streams of lower manhattan and
built over them   at great cost too   because in order to
    build there the developers had to pump out the water to
make sure that the buildings they built didnt sink into the
streams that ran under the streets   you find out about this
now every time you build a new expensive high rise and
discover that the foundations are in contention with the
water that refuses to go away

            so the city was teeming and filthy and reeking
    and what you had was a population of white slaves living

130

in southern manhattan as you had a population of black slaves
living south of the mason dixon line   white slaves living
under a slightly different form of slavery   which olmsted
who was a profoundly committed anti-slavery person
felt was impossible for citizens of a republic   and
olmsted believed that you needed to do a great number of
things to turn slaves into citizens   it wouldnt be enough
to release them into poverty and indifference and dirt to
create citizens of a republic   which he imagined you could
do
and maybe you cant but olmsted imagined you could   maybe
we still dont have citizens and maybe we dont have a republic
but in 1858 or 1857 olmsted thought you could   and
there were other people who thought so too   or thought you
had to try   for whatever reasons   and they   olmsted and
vaux   created this image   of nature   an artifice
representing a benevolent and subtly civilized nature
north of the city   where they imagined people going to
become free citizens   free and responsible

and to help them be free and responsible olmsted
hired a large police force that he placed inside the park
realizing that if he didnt have a police force there he
might very soon not have a park   as the peoples baser
instincts might emerge before nature had its chance to
civilize them   and the city would have a disaster on its
hands   which at times weve had in central park   the
police notwithstanding

and looking at central park   at its images of a
kind of humanly scaled nature that laid claim to being
exemplary   functional and exemplary   looking at it   you
realize that its a beautiful and marvelous failure   not
at being a park but at civilizing its citizenry   its a
great failure   which was not the fault of the park or its
designers   because what they wanted couldnt have worked
not in this way   and though a park can do a lot of great
things it doesnt create citizens   a wordsworthian
enterprise does not create citizens   not by itself
on the other hand it does a lot and i was surprised
to see in a recent report made by a group of people who were

131

examining the park and trying to see what use it had   that
not only do a wide variety of people from all over the city
make use of the park   but that something like 68% of the
people who come to the park   which they know by whatever
method they tag and count those people   turn out to be
solitaries who come to the park to be there alone   so it
may not make citizens but it may make certain ways of being
meditatively human more possible   it may restore a special
way of being human for brief intervals   maybe thats one of
the things it can do in its way

but the park is always under assault   like the
land in general   like the land of the hudson valley
which has always been under assault   its been under
assault from the industries that dump garbage into it
willingly or unwillingly
i know they dont always do it on
purpose but only because its cheaper   and sometimes they
dont even know what theyre doing   usually they dont really
know what theyre doing   and all the undesirable things
wind up in the river
coming up the river i was surprised at
how much dumping goes on along the edge   i was surprised
at how many ruined cars are dumped there   its very curious
how many cars get into strange places fragments of cars   so
many car bodies stripped of almost everything   you wonder
how they got down there and what was carried off   cars
minus axles minus motors minus interior upholstery lying
there like flayed carcasses   flayed somewhere north of
rye
they increase in frequency as you get between rye and
here   and all those dumpings of odd sorts of things
mattresses mattress springs torn fragments of things
strips of hanging things like body bags from the vietnamese
war   black plastic sacks dangling from an embankment
and you wonder what was in it a corpse or old clothes
and why this dumping right at the edge of the hudson
its not as if its always easy to get down there   but its
the anonymous place where the land breaks down

its as if somehow the cut that the water makes into

the land creates a space thats not anybodys   its as if
everyone knows that nobody can take possession of it that
uncertain terrain sometimes soggy and sometimes flooded
     smelling of rotting weeds   or debris cast off by the river
itself   the cut that the water makes into the land creates
     at its edge an unpredictable place that is absolutely
     unownable   so maybe the carelessness with which its
     treated is a sign of some insight into the fact that its not
ownable   because its not surveyable usable or even reliably
     navigable   sometimes under water sometimes emerging from
it slippery indeterminable its a no mans land   except in
     the few places where they have these little boat basins most
     of them pretty shabby at that   and i passed one of them
     that was pretty dilapidated   it must have been an old boat
yard and there was this really run down lopsided old barge
with shingle roofing   that sported in dirty white lettering
     on its side the proud sign   HUDSON YACHT CLUB

          i suppose it was a joke   that the barge was an
old garbage scow that had been beached along the shore that
somebody had found some use for in some stupid business of no
     great consequence but decided in a fit of humor to lay
     claim to it   while the other side of the river the
western side declared itself more proudly in giant
     enterprises   fortresses along the rhine   a vast power
     plant thriving on lethal fuel   a great space invaders
fortress with impregnable walls looking out on a subjugated
     planet for which the conquerors intend no likely good   and
     here was the shabby hudson   a grey cut in the countryside
          and you realize that the river is in a way the beginning
of the land
                    traveling up the river you have a sense of it as
     the beginning   the way it determines the geography and
ecology of the space   and the flood plain of the river is a
     kind of central place for the region   and that without
the river there would have been very little   without this
     glacial cut that it must have been all the way down to the
sea there would be no hudson valley   and it is a strange
beginning for a place   though nothing ever begins of course

          i mean you know how rivers begin in the sea and end

in the sea after an interval in the air   and theres this
ongoing cycle you know about and you cant cut the beginning
loose from the end or tell them apart   but you realize
that your own sense of it is different   because you always
look for an onset in the highlands   you look for the
headwaters   of the nile   and you wonder what dirty
spring system polluted by what chemical plant that makes what
kind of toxic thing   or what filthy snow filled with what
poisonous waste lies on the hillsides of the headwaters of
the hudson   you think of alan moorehead writing about the
search for the headwaters of the nile   only now we dont
conduct that kind of search in the same way   now we want
to find what dioxin plant sits there on top and is sending
its effluents down river to greet the shad   and you figure
the two will come together somewhere around here   at
poughkeepsie

    but beginnings   seem not to really happen that
way   i know there are places that feel as though they
could be beginnings   and then its too late because the
beginning has happened already   you look at the countryside
of the hudson and you say its too late   and in a way thats
a mistake because its always too late   and its always too
early   its always too early to do anything   about the
things that have to be done   but on the other hand its
always too late to do it too   and everybody can always
explain to you why its too late and why its too early
  except that the beginning always has to be somewhere in
the middle
      and if you try to explain it to yourself   as i
tried to explain to myself what i was doing there
contemplating the idaho schist on the floor of my brother-
and sister-in-laws apartment looking out at the manhattan
schist outcrops twenty-seven floors below   and wondering
why they were leaving the idaho schist   it seemed to me i
was thinking of myself being displaced from new york
  which i always considered my city   as i wandered off
to california

    i wandered out there by accident   though in a
sense everything ive ever done has been by accident   and

maybe also on purpose   accidental purpose
                                    i wound up in
california by accident   i had no desire to go to california
to san diego   if somebody had ever said to me in 1950
     you know you may wind up living in san diego   i would
have said go away indianapolis is more likely   san diego
stood to me   as a new yorker   i was almost going to say
as an american   as an impossibility   the idea of it was
preposterous   as if san diego was a street in the center of
which an admiral stood greeting all arrivals   at least a
 chief petty officer
                              it didnt seem to me that anyone in his
right mind would ever want to live in san diego   except
maybe sailors or mexican workers   i didnt even think of
them as living in san diego   i thought of it as a
retirement home for shoestore owners from indiana and
 nebraska   and when i got there in 1968 it turned out that
san diego was the place that indiana and arkansas went to
retire or open furniture stores or restaurants and they
 brought all the excellences of wichita and indianapolis
cuisine to san diego   where it combined with the cuisine of
kentucky and virginia   which added sugar to it and i
thought this was really a very strange place i hardly knew
what to make of it

            san diego is like the end of the united states and
 its really very beautiful in a strange way   but it was
beautiful before they got here from kansas and oklahoma
     part of it they neglected and that has remained
beautiful   but what they didnt neglect hasnt remained
beautiful   because they decided that san diego was on the
 mediterranean   they had a strange sense of geography
     they decided they had landed on the algerian coast   so
they put up palm trees date palms   but they also imported
 korean grass and bougainvillea and australian sweet gum
 trees   and after a generation of feeding these exotic
blooms with water from the north they began to think of them
as native flora   and the australian eucalyptus flourished

        they had imported it in the 1880s to provide ties
 for the railroad   and its wood was not good enough   but

135

southern california is a lot like the australian desert
so the eucalyptus flourished anyway   and the farmers
thought to use rows of eucalyptus as windbreaks for their
mediterranean orange trees   which didnt flourish without
the provision of lots and lots of water   because san diego
is very much like the australian desert   in which it rains
rarely and heavily   that is when it rains it often rains
heavily but it is a rare occasion
from june to october it
almost never rains   hardly a drop of rain   there is sun
and sun and more sun except for an overcast morning or
evening   and there isnt a drop of rain for months on end
this untroubled place dries and dries and dries   yet
trees flourish   luxuriant palms and jacaranda and orange
trees and olives   green tentacles extend all over san
diego   supported by water coming down from the north or
from the east   which they send down to grow these strange
things that they exhibit to tourists as the native thing
because now nearly nobody remembers what native forms there
were   except in a few places spotted irregularly around the
county
we live on a patch of native growth   three acres of
chaparral   you let it alone and it grows   we live on
three acres of it it keeps people away because its like a
thicket and its marvelously fragrant and hospitable for
birds coyotes and small deer and we like it   but we're on
the outside   and being on the outside is like being at the
beginning

i got to san diego and i didnt know i wanted to
join it   i suppose i wanted to be there i didnt have to be
there and i was there   it was an accident   somebody said
to me how would you like to come teach in san diego   i
thought it was as reasonable to teach in san diego as
anywhere
theres no reason not to teach in san diego   what
should i have said to him   no i dont want to teach in san
diego   the question was did i want to teach   i wasnt
thrilled by the idea but it was intriguing for a moment to
think of teaching   i hadnt done any teaching i had done

a lot of other things   and now somebody suggested teaching
     and i thought it over and it was a possibility   and i was
persuaded to go out there and teach

              and there wasnt much there   a few concrete
     buildings and the remains of an old military camp   which
had been turned into a university with the help of a
     checkbook   and there it was   the regents of the
university of california had taken over some thousand or
more acres that had once belonged to the marines when it was
     camp matthews and they joined it to a powerful oceanographic
research institute and made it into a high powered science
     university that required a certain degree of respectability
     and i was there to help give it that respectability   which
     i thought was very funny
                              they brought me in to add a certain
cultural respectability   because you cant let scientists
all alone by themselves   theres no telling what they might
do   so what you do is bring in people from the arts and
     humanities so they might feel ashamed
                                   or they might feel
     gratified and flattered and beneficent   so that you would
stand in the corner of their nuclear reactor and they would
     feel better   and then they would make gifts to you and
you could make art and art would go on the walls of the
nuclear reactor or whatever else they were constructing
     so i thought that was an amusing way to live   weve
been court jesters before   and i took the opportunity to
go out there and found out it was not really like that   in
those days there were more scientists   scientists who were
     really scientists not mere number crunchers   now we have
more technicians than we used to   then there were actually
many cultivated men and women in the sciences out there
     the engineers hadnt arrived yet and the numerical
analysts   and lots of the scientists were educated some
were from europe and they could even converse and had
certainly read   we dont have many of those left now   the
     young ones are not like that at all   theyre completely
barbaric and wonderful its a generation of visigoths and
     what we need now is a new wulfilas to write them a

                                             137

testament in their language that will reenact st peter
   cutting off the tax collectors ear in a dramatic enough way
   to get some conversions   and then we can start working
again   but in the meantime a race of brilliant technicians
has replaced the scientists   many of whom have retired
      or gone on to other places   and its a sad state of
affairs   that we're dealing with cheerfully because what
else can we do

                     we're certainly rich we're affluent   which
is always nice even in a war type economy   a science
university   its nice to be rich   so we're rich   we're
rich and we're dangerous   and we sit there being rich and
dangerous and talk about the dangers of our richness   and
we have a chancellor who is a wonderfully handsome little
man who has white hair and looks like a child who sits
under a sunlamp every day and is infinitely charming to
ladies and developers and bankers from whom he brings in
lots and lots of money to build us the ugliest buildings in
all san diego   and he does this out of a prodigious good
will   with which he defaces the landscape of eucalyptus
that are not native but are the only trees the university
has got   and he has built us prestige after prestige   and
gradually destroyed the environment with these buildings
      and he does this with the best will in the world
      theres nothing you can say to him about this   i know
because weve tried   and when you explain it to him   that
these buildings are appalling   he says what would you have
me do   if i couldnt build this building now i wouldnt
ever be able to build it again   and if we say then dont
build it ever he doesnt seem to be able to hear

            one of the science buildings is just now about to
be built on what was until now a very attractlve meadowlike
space   and the faculty   much of the faculty   even some
of the science faculty   except for the biology and
chemistry departments   were in a state of rage about them
putting this tall building there and defacing one of the nice
green areas when they had hundreds of acres they could put
it on elsewhere
               so we said do we have to put it there   why

138

do you have to put it there   our school prides itself on
being a democracy   so this was at an academic senate
meeting where almost everything winds up getting discussed
     so we said why do you have to put it there   and they
answered "so that the coastal winds can dissipate the
pollution from its stacks"   so you can see its hard to get
anywhere in a rational way   and it always feels like we're
dealing with some kind of crazy beginning there   we're
always starting to fight battles to stand off this
continuous eating away at the place

          recently a number of us tried to present a plan for
them to treat the land the environment we live in   in a
more respectful way
                    there is a very attractive park in san
diego   once olmsted and vaux created the germinal park of
the united states   which was central park and then prospect
park   the park movement caught on   and nearly every city
in the country had to have its park and the one they have
here is a very pretty spanish looking park called balboa
park   naturally after one of the conquistadors   and it
was built up at the time of the great columbian exposition
at the turn of the century with lots of stucco and spanish
tile buildings in the style of a new spain colonial fantasy
     and there are several museums down there and a zoo and
lots of green lawns and tall palm trees   and its a very
nice looking park situated not far from the center of
downtown san diego about twelve miles south of the university
     which is up on a mesa overlooking the pacific ocean and
la jolla
          and we tried to sell them the administration of the
university on the hope of trying to save the universitys
thousand or so acres by thinking of it as a kind of park
          and i came up with this term in the hope they might like
it and find comfort in it   and i suggested that they try
to turn the university of california san diego into an
academic park   whats an academic park   i dont know but
i had some hope for them liking it based on an analogy
principle with an industrial park   which was something
theyd heard of and could approve of   and i guessed they

might imagine it sounded a little like a science park only a
little more general
                              i suppose i could have said a
philosophical park but that would have killed it altogether
    but i figured theyd know that an academy was a good
place because thats where you get grants   so we suggested
to them that what we really needed was an academic park
that would be a model to the community of an ecologically
humane place that would set an example in how to build and
above all not build when natural conditions required it   a
place that would inspire with its surroundings a discourse
with nature and graceful ways of living within and around it
that would let the ravens continue to nest in our buildings
and the hawks and leave the coyotes enough breeding space
and the little iguana and deer   we have an awful lot of
land   and i thought under that emblem we might be able to
protect it

                    and we made this suggestion to them   and while we
were working out this suggestion they kept eating away at the
landscape   they said oh its a good idea   chomp chomp
    chomp   and they put up a building here   they knocked
down trees there   we said why did you have to knock down
five hundred and fifty trees to build the student center
    we have so much land and we have so very few big groves
of trees and we had this beautiful grove of eucalyptus right
across from the only attractive building on the campus
    which was the library   a kind of science fiction
looking building out of concrete and glass shaped like a slide
projector designed for communication with extraterrestrials
    a lovely impractical building surrounded in its charming
preposterousness by a splendid grove of eucalyptus trees

                    one day we got there at the end of the summer and
the trees were gone in their place were these amputated
stumps five hundred and fifty stumps of living eucalyptus
trees weird looking little tables   and theyd gone through
there and put little red flags up near them to show that this
was no accident   we'd tried to get them to turn this place
into an academic park and theyd turned it into a field of
carnage   we'd even promised to design a lake in a

140

godforsaken eroded spot that would draw on the natural
    drainage system and we'd proposed a variety of pleasant
things that people could deal with

                                theres a sculpture program
here   a good one called the stuart collection   thats
placed radical sculptural constructions all about the campus
    we would integrate this with various walks and groves
and circles and knolls   we would work this all out   but
    there was no time   as always it was too late to begin
        or too early   they said were not ready for this yet so
    it was too early   then they said it was too late because
the trees were already destroyed and the plans for the space
    already made   so it was also too late   and once again
we were between too early and too late   and to this day my
wife is mad on this subject   shes on one of the powerful
    committees that never have any power   this committee with
a very great title   shes a professor here and shes an
    artist and people like her   they think shes a marvelous
lunatic artist   and she goes around pounding on peoples
desks saying how can you let this happen   and they say
    eleanor youre right   and it continues to happen   the
chancellor likes her and invites her to breakfast and she
says how can you let this happen   and he says eleanor how
    could i stop it   and its like punching a pillow

            we're constantly aware that what we're dealing with
    is like being in a chute   its like a chute and we're
falling in it   and maybe its like being in a river and
    we're being swept out to sea   but we're not sure whether
    we're being swept out to the ocean or sucked into the
bottom of some very foul swamp   because at least if its the
    ocean you figure   california will lead america over the
cliff and everything will fall in   and thats one of the
    reasons for praising california architecture   i know a lot
    of people praise california architecture   what they like
    about it is its lightness   it looks as if   if you move
your hand quickly you could knock it into the sea
                                            and theres
    something consoling about this lack of permanence   as if
its damage is only temporary and not enduring   and its not

built for the ages   because the people have no faith in
ages existing   and they may be right   there may not be
ages existing if they continue to build this way

now this sense of being swept   of being swept up
and away   it seems to me that it still doesnt make you feel
hopeless   theres a paradox in this   theres a paradox
that for all of this im cheerful   i bring you good news of
disaster   its a disaster i refuse to be depressed about
because what difference would it make if i was depressed
i know that i was a very bad leftist as a kid because i
wasnt sufficiently depressed

the history of the american left
had two psychological forms   one growing out of its
sensitivity to the wrongs suffered by innumerable victims was
a profound glumness   the other which sometimes accompanied
this grew out of a humorless sense of the importance of their
mission   and their sense of everyone elses responsibility
and seemed to involve a mental construction akin to a
kinetic sculpture   that it seemed to me almost all their
writing turned into   something like a single long finger
wagging in strong disapproval   and i suppose i wasnt much
good at either of these   and as for the american right
nobody can take it seriously   unless you have a kind of
kamikaze-like playfulness and are for the sport of it willing
to follow william buckley over a cliff

but given our alternatives it seems to me you may
as well be cheerful even though things are pretty bad
because things have always been bad   you know i used to
believe there must have been golden days once   it took me
a long time to get over this belief   but im over it now
and i figure there was always a bad situation that you took
on more or less well   and if it somehow started out fine
you would come to the bad scene pretty soon bye and bye
and i think of my father-in-law   as a man for whom
things started out fine   so fine he can never stop telling
you the story of his great beginning   and now his
situation is not so fine but he's ninety years old and he's
learned how to face it with the ongoing charm of a man
who's been living so long he's gotten quite good at it

142

now he's ninety years old and we meet to play
tennis   and i suppose thats already a sign of a good
    situation   or at least the way that he plays it is a sign
of the way that he lives with it

        im not a very competitive tennis player because it
    takes too much time and effort if you want to play it that
way   so im a good partner for my father-in-law   who has
    always been a kind of elegant player with easy looking
    strokes and he likes to keep diffidently returning the ball
        and if i dont hit it too far   because he's lost some
of his mobility he always gets it back to me very prettily
    because he has elegant ground strokes   so i dont knock
    myself out and i keep playing with him and i enjoy the
    cheerfulness of his game and i enjoy having him instruct me
        being ninety years old he always gives me tennis lessons
        he tells me how i could improve my serve   he tells me
how my backhand could get more top spin on it   and he
    interrupts the game any number of times and he does this to
everybody

            if there are people on the neighboring court he'll
give them advice too   especially pretty young women and
even young men   who seem to enjoy hearing quaint tennis
lore from a slender old gentleman with a small pointed beard
    and courtly ways   even though it slows up everybodys game
        but his idea of the game goes back to borotra and rene
lacoste and has a strong esthetic component because he's a
painter and a poet living here in san diego   which i
    suppose is not so strange   because there are plenty of
poets and painters living in san diego   but peter happens
    to be a serious ninety year old hungarian poet and painter
    living here in san diego   and thats where his situation
is not so fine   because what good is hungarian poetry
    in san diego and what good is it to be a very good and
idiosyncratic and unfamous painter when youre ninety years
    old even if you have shows

            but once peter was famous   or felt famous for a
very short time   and it was at the very beginning   and
    then he was famous again   not so famous as before but for
    a longer period of time   but what he remembers most and

cant ever forget is the story of his beginning   a beginning
that was so blessed it took him completely by surprise   and
to this day i dont think he can quite understand it   which
is why i think he's told it to me so many times

                 peter   his real name was joszef   joszef barna
or barna joszef the way they say it in hungarian   was a
bright young jewish kid from the provinces with a gift for
his own language and some drawing talent   and because his
father was a craftsman   a painter of church interiors with
formulaic christs and angels and lots of gold in the little
town of keckemet   and because he had an older brother who
had a job in a bank in budapest   and because he'd done well
in the gymnasium they sent him to study architecture in the
capital   where he painted delicate water colors and
wrestled with projective geometry and read poetry and wrote
tortured stories about sexual experiences he had never had
          violent stories about squalid relations between a
hunchbacked woman and a dwarf in an environment of abject
poverty   about a high school boy going mad on his first
trip to a local whorehouse   stories that peter   remembers
now   because they were filled with lurid atmosphere and
fantastical events and written in a language wild with fear
and loathing and compassion   as surrealistic   but i think
might be better described as expressionist because it was
1914 or '15 and this was very much the sense of the time

          and as young barna joszef had written three of
these stories he showed them to a friend   who was a
student at the university   who was so impressed by these
fantasies that he showed them to his professor   who it
turned out was a man named babits   who peter assured me was
after ady and someone else whose name i cant remember   the
number 3 poet of all hungary   and it just so happened an
editor of *nyugat*
                    and it was with babits   the number 3 poet
of all hungary that these stories sat and sat and sat   till
peter   still joszef   then became restless and finally
persuaded his friend to find out what had become of his
stories   and then as the often repeated story goes   the
editor of *nyugat*   the great hungarian magazine founded by

144

ady to face "west"   which was its name (nyugat means west)
    from hungarian ground   the chief editor   a man named
oszvat   a distinguished critic and scholar   and not
  babits the number 3 poet who had sat on peters stories all
  this time and had now finally passed them onto this man
      oszvat the chief editor summoned peter to the journals
offices to warn him sternly to care for his talent that he
most surely could not understand   and to inform him that he
  was going to print not one but all three of the stories in
    successive issues of the magazine

        now can you imagine what this must have been like
at the age of eighteen   to be picked up by your countrys
  leading literary magazine   it was like being picked up by
  an eagle   and in the intoxication of his flight barna
  joszef changed his name to moor peter or peter moor
                                                    now   to
speakers of english this may not sound like very much   we
  might think of the wistful songs of thomas moore and "all
  those endearing young charms" or the bleak moors of scotland
      but for the slender and delicately handsome young poet
  he was assuming a name that called to mind the
  smoldering moor of venice   thats what an eagles flight can
  do   and peter seems to have remained in the air for quite
  a long time   waiting for his story to appear and soared
even higher after it came out   though it appears that an
uncle of his who set a lot of store by his own literary
  sensibility got angry with him for not revealing to him
  anything of this great hidden talent   but under the name
  of moor peter rapidly made the acquaintance of the small
glittering art society of budapest in which he was celebrated
as a kind of golden youth whose star was rising   and all
  through the great war   from which he was excused because
  of a condition like asthma   he remained in budapest and
  wrote and was widely admired by the artistic society of
cultivated men and lovely sensitive ladies for the one story
  he had published in the great literary magazine   so much
  so that he withdrew from the architectural school where the
  mathematics was troubling him anyway   and prepared to lead
  the literary life

145

               but publication was slow in *nyugat*   it
was an older magazine   its editors were busy men   there
was a war on   the finances were uncertain   and then the
government collapsed and reformed under count carolyi   and
the magazine temporarily suspended operations   meanwhile
peter got engaged to an attractive young pianist and waited
for the appearance of his second story   for which he had
already checked the proofs   and then the carolyi regime
collapsed and then reformed briefly as a communist
government under bela kun   and oszvat   *nyugats* chief
editor took an administrative position in the commune and
the magazine   which had seemed on the point of resuming
operations   discontinued them   so peter took a minor job
as a censor with the new government and waited some more
       then came admiral horthys right wing coup bela kun fled
and there was a general roundup of liberal and left wing
intellectuals

         peter as a minor functionary of the left wing
government and a jew got arrested and thrown into a jail
    where he was held for a while at the local police
station   a notorious place where people were interrogated
and tortured before being sent off to detention or execution
    because the horthy government quickly made itself known
for violence and nastiness   and peter was beaten up and
questioned   and he has terrible memories of that jail
    where people he knew were tortured in unspeakable ways
and sent off to their death   and he tells the story of
standing in a room filled with other prisoners waiting to be
sent off from one detention place to another and seeing a
   man that he knew who had been horribly violated and was now
nearly unrecognizable in a state of shock leaning against a
wall   when a dandyish young officer and a beautiful woman
in evening clothes swept into the room   they had been
dancing and they were still slightly drunk and laughing   and
they suddenly stopped   and the officer looked around and
pointed to the exhausted prisoner and said "that man is a
communist"   and the woman went up and stared at him pulled
her cape around her and spat in the mans face
                  but peter was

146

lucky because an old school friend an aristocrat wandered
    into the police station spotted him there and used some
influence to get him out

        so peter slipped down the river to vienna where he
was safe   but here his situation was not so fine   he was
no longer a rising star   he was simply another hungarian
emigre whose german was not so good   who had no profession
and now had a wife   he had married the young pianist and
now they were poor emigrés together   she gave piano lessons
and he got a few jobs as an extra in films made by a
hungarian director   and life was pretty miserable for him
there in vienna   it was as if somehow the eagle that had
picked him up and flown with him toward olympus had suddenly
dropped him at the foot of a barren mountain slope where he
was now wandering around trying to get his bearings

        so they emigrated to the united states where his
wife had relatives
                    now he had spoken poor german but he had
no english at all   and he was still further from the
literary world he had known in budapest   and he had to
start a life as a craftsman doing lettering and signs for
local merchants while his wife taught piano high up in the
upper heights of northern manhattan   where he lived for a
long time as a quaint emigré with a charming accent
    preparing signs during the day and writing at night in
hungarian   long novels that there was no audience for   or
a very small audience because he managed to find here in
manhattan a hungarian emigré community in exile   hungry for
their native language and culture
                            so peter was suddenly
discovered again by an antifascist hungarian newspaper and
by hungarian radio   and he wrote articles and stories for
the one and read poems for the other   and he was something
of a star once again   this time in a smaller emigré
community   or maybe it was even the same size   who knows
how big the literary community of budapest was before 1920
    and he lived by his commercial art during the day and
wrote during the night and was a lion of new yorks hungarian
emigré community and his wife left him and he was happy

or cheerful as he expressed the painful struggles of the
citys poor in the great depression   and denounced the rise
of the nazis in brilliantly rhymed folkish ballads that he
explained to me were not so modern as what he had written
before but just as good and maybe better to reach the people
    which he had never thought about before

        and maybe they were   i cant tell   i only know
a few sentences of hungarian and snatches of verse   peter
had promised to teach me once   but he was a terrible
teacher and i never had the time   so i cant really tell
    but for the community of hungarian emigrés living in
new york they were eloquent and powerful poems   and many
years later a hungarian scholar came over who was researching
the emigré writers and collected peters texts and wrote an
article about him for a journal published by the magyar
academy of sciences   so i suppose they were eloquent and
powerful if traditional poems   but after the war the
second world war things were different   all through the
thirties and forties you write these poems denouncing horthy
and fascism   and then horthy and the fascists are swept
away and you suddenly have nothing to do

        i suppose peter was exhausted   i imagine he could
have gone back to hungary   to budapest and tried to pick up
his career again   if you can call it that   as a hungarian
writer   and he went over there after the war   to see if
    that was what he wanted to do   but the hungarians werent
interested in him   somehow the last issue of *nyugat* in
which his first story was published hadnt been widely
distributed and had gotten lost   the other one that had
been set up in proofs had disappeared   nobody really knew
him or wanted to know him   he was just another hungarian
emigré and peter wasnt sure that he wanted to be there
anyway   his mother was dead   his brother was dead
    killed by the nazis just before theyd pulled out   most
of his friends were gone   only his sister marika remained
    and peter had been living in the united states so long
that maybe he was no longer a hungarian writer but an
american hungarian writer   so he turned around and came
home and cheerfully became a painter

148

            or maybe not so cheerfully and only gradually   he
had always painted   slight watercolors   impressionist
landscapes that he painted on trips he took with his
   hungarian friends to the adirondacks or the rockies   and
   he'd painted watercolors in architecture school   so he
returned to the watercolors   and they became more elaborate
as he worked them over with inks and chalks   and the
   surfaces became more ambiguous and the images became more
   fantastical   underseascapes with exotic fronds twisting
roots and menacing shapes   sunken rock structures vaguely
resembling monsters or titans   and they became surreal

         among his hungarian friends there were one or two
painters to whom he showed his paintings   and they
encouraged him to enter them in shows sponsored by watercolor
   societies or associations of american artists   and his
   paintings were accepted and exhibited   and he won a few
   prizes and he was awarded a medal by a museum in new jersey
         and he really was cheerful and somewhat surprised to be
accepted by this small world   in which i think he regarded
himself at first as something of an imposter because he
   wasnt formally trained and had no understanding of anatomy
or perspective   because he was really a poet   and he
continued to write stories and poems at the same time   but
in english now because he had married again my mother-in-law
         a passionate dark haired little woman of russian and
   polish extraction   and she didnt know any hungarian   only
russian and polish and english   so he eventually got tired
of reading his marvelous sounding hungarian poetry to her
      because it was as unintelligible to her as pushkin was
to him   but she was a wonderfully appreciative audience for
his fantastical stories of paintings that came alive in the
   metropolitan museum at night   rubens horsemen riding·down
   5th avenue and up 53rd street to shoot arrows into the
cezannes on the walls of the museum of modern art   but
   even more for his dreamy and menacing watercolors   that
she never got tired of studying and criticizing and admiring

         and as he continued to make more paintings that they
   argued about and admired together   he began to consider
himself more of a painter than a poet   and because jeanette

was an energetic and gregarious woman she encouraged him
to exhibit his paintings and arranged a couple of shows for
him in small but respectable new york galleries   for which
he received some friendly reviews in the newspapers and art
magazines   and he began to regard himself somewhat more
confidently as a painter   and even then in his fifties he
might have made a kind of cheerful career for himself as a
painter   only he simply had no idea of how to do it

because he had this idea of beginnings from his
early days back in hungary   an idea of being picked up by
an eagle and soaring   and making a career as a painter
meant even in this little world   besides making paintings
and entering shows   going to openings and talking to other
artists and gallery owners and joining associations and
going to meetings and generally   hanging around and
becoming part of a world   and i made the mistake a number of
years later when i got to know him and peters paintings had
become even more elaborate and fantastical in style as well
as subject matter   of introducing him to betty parsons
who was still running a serious gallery then   and she
came down with her gallery director   who was jock truman i
think   to their dark apartment off central park and studied
the paintings and looked interested and said little   but
invited peter to come down and visit the gallery   which
peter never did   because he was slightly offended that
they hadnt praised his paintings   and jeanette was a little
resentful that they had declined her cookies and tea   and
they never went down to the gallery and were a little
irritated with me   because what they didnt understand was
that peter was supposed to go down to the gallery and see a
few shows and bring down new work   and generally talk to
the gallery people and hang around and give them enough time
to get used to the work   so that they could finally feel
comfortable with it and give peter a show

but peter knew how to make paintings even if he
didnt know how to make a career   and he continued to make
them as long as he could show them to jeanette for her to
argue with him and admire them   and the paintings got even
more bizarre and wonderful when peter and jeanette followed

150

us out to san diego   where he fell in love with the
sunlight and exotic flora and fanciful architecture of
southern california   which he abstracted in the paintings
into evocations of tropical architectures and cliff
   structures floating or drowned in luminous atmospheres
      and he painted so rapidly and well that then in his
middle eighties   he filled two one man shows in two
successive years in san diego   with over forty new
paintings   and he would still be painting cheerfully now

         but as they both got older jeanettes mind started
to fail   her memory went   and she panicked and grew
   frightened and angry and was no longer a good audience for
every new painting   because she couldnt remember what she
had seen or said   and she got furious to be reminded of
   what she forgot and she bit him and kicked him in the
shins   and finally had to go into an old age home where
she could afford to forget that she had forgotten   and
   peter was no longer a painter again

         he had the paintings they were all around him
   but he was no longer painting new ones and he was deeply
depressed   for a while   but then he started to read again
      and one day he was reading a hungarian literary magazine
that we'd brought back from new york for him   and he came
on a long poem by a new hungarian poet that struck him as so
new and so modern that he started to translate it
                                                    which may
seem like a strange activity for this 90 year old hungarian
emigré who had never really mastered idiomatic english and
had to have his own poems and stories translated for him
      but peters english written english was serviceable
enough when he was moved by a feeling to write   not
serviceable enough perhaps to translate his own hungarian
   stories and poems   because there he was moved too deeply
by his own hungarian impulses   but serviceable enough to
   translate someone elses hungarian impulses   and it was a
long and fractured work about a kind of existential christ
      and the hungarian was difficult and its vocabulary was
technological and sacramental   but peter worked cheerfully
   at it for a long time and finally finished it   and then he

didnt know what to do with it

so he sent it to hungary to the hungarian poet by
way of the magazine   and sent him also some of his own
hungarian poems the rhyming antifascist poems from his days
with the emigré magazine   by way of introduction   and
then he waited a very long time for an answer

and while he
waited he began to write again   in hungarian   he began
composing a novella   dealing with his childhood   and he
got very happy writing down memories from those times in
keckemet   and he read small portions of it to us in
fractured translations which always dissatisfied him   but
he kept on writing at it   and finally the hungarian poet
wrote back

he was clearly flattered that peter had translated
his poem   but pointed out that it had been translated into
english before and told him in what magazine   and he
thanked him for the translation   but of peters own poems
he made no mention at all and   of course being a modernist
poet in budapest in nineteen eighty-three or -four   with
russia not nazi germany breathing over his shoulder   what
could he have made of those rhyming antifascist poems of
1943 or '44

so now peter has stopped writing again   and he's
stopped but in a way he's still cheerful   and he's reading
again   this time in english   not goethe   but stendhal
again   novels of young men and their desires   and he
looks with desire at attractive young women and with delight
at children and babies   he strolls about the streets of
la jolla taking in with pleasure the exotic plantings and
the crystalline air   and he still has his writings and
paintings gathered around him   and he still takes his
slides around to the galleries   where the gallery owners
often admire them   because the paintings are admirable
but what can the galleries do with them   theyre in
business to make money   and peter is a very good and
unfamous painter who is 90 years old   and a 90 year old
painter has to be famous   because he cant be promising

any more

      so he's gone back to reading stendhal and kurt
vonnegut   who he tells me is very good but too smart to be
a very great writer   and we talk about them   and he likes
to tell me about goethe   who he thinks is very great but
knows i have no taste for   so we sit in chinese restaurants
and yell at each other cheerfully because his hearing is not
very good   about goethe and stendhal and sometimes about
  vonnegut and nabokov   and sometimes he complains about
the hungarians for not valuing his poems and stories and
reminds me of his great beginning how he was picked up by the
  eagle and dropped on the way to the mountain

      and still he has his paintings and writings
gathered around him   and he plays tennis and walks out in
the sunlight and he's ninety years old   and he has his
sense of the meaningfulness and strangeness of his work
strangely collected here in san diego   and when he dies it
will probably be no stranger than most things in this
environment at all

it was late november and i had just finished giving a
couple of talks in buffalo   and since i was there for the
first time   like most visitors i wanted to see the falls at
niagara   john minkowsky   who was then director of the
media studies center   drove me out there though the weather
had suddenly become brutally cold and the falls were frozen
over into a great sheet of ice glistening under a triple
rainbow   i tried to locate the place where the diaghilev
dancer who'd emigrated to the united states and become
despondent at american indifference had leaped to his death
      i thought i'd found it though i had to go out some
distance beyond the fencing to photograph it for eleanor
      who was preparing her antinova recollections at the
time   and it was with a sense of success that john and i
were driving back in his old volkswagen when i glimpsed from
      the freeway the astonishingly graceful statue of some civil
war hero poised above the snow in a mild contraposto like
some manet drawing room dandy in a green suit   but john who
was driving hadnt seen it and had no idea who the sculptor
was or the dandy   and we had no time to go back and find
out because i had a bus to catch for toronto   which i
      arrived at with just a couple of hours to spare before my
talk at the ontario art center   where i caught a glimpse
of the obligatory henry moore out in front of the museum and
went off to my motel till the time of the performance

      in the room i reflected on the curiousness of the fact
that the subject of the museums exhibition that had brought
me out there was autobiography in film and video   while
the conversation in buffalo the night before with gerry

155

grady and stan brakhage had been all about the way
structuralism had taken over all independent filmmaking
     so with my mind playing over the twin subjects of
autobiography and structuralism i came to the conclusion
described in the letter i wrote eleanor before going off to
my performance

                                        5:30 pm   nov 30 1978
dear eleanor

i have at length decided to tell the story of anastasius and
genya   the red haired dwarf painter and his eurasian girl
friend model and muse   the story is one i have been
reluctant to tell for some time because its inherent high
color gives it in an age where fact is suggested by a low
key palette an air of low credibility   but because
autobiography calls for truth rather than plausibility and
because the experience was a meaningful part of my life at a
period when i had no clear idea of the relationship between
tonality and truth   and because of the extreme timeliness
of his linguistic   if i may say structuralist impulse
that i am afraid went lost in an earlier period   ive
persuaded myself to overcome my own reluctance and tell his
florid tale—

                                        david

* this will be my last piece on the trip

the structuralist

the occasion for my coming to speak was an
autobiography exhibition in a toronto museum consisting
mainly of works in film and video   and because this was a
museum   i could tell from the henry moore outside the main
entry way that this situation must have been somewhat
surprising for my audience on two counts   that it was
autobiography they were being asked to consider   by way of
film and video   and that this was being asked of them in
an art museum   where people are certainly more used to
looking at paintings and sculptures of an abstract or
structuralist sort   though this was a contemporary art
museum and the year was 1978

and while it was fairly recent
for young artists   sculptors painters video makers
photographers and performance people   to be taking up
autobiography in a deliberate and self-conscious way   and
something new for them   it was not so new for filmmakers
and not so fashionable in the world of independent cinema
where younger artists seemed to be working out a kind of
structuralist film   quite similar to the sort of sculpture
and painting that used to be popular among young artists in
new york about ten or twelve years earlier   while young
new york artists were by then pretty tired of that and were
taking a new look at autobiography in some of the ways that
had been popular with some independent filmmakers about
fifteen or twenty years earlier

now if at first this may seem a little puzzling
this coming and going of interests so apparently
distinct they appear arbitrary or merely trivial   like the
cycle of fashion where caprice may dictate long skirts and

dark colors and natural fabrics one year   or short skirts
and bright colors and plastics the next   even fashion has
 a logic of a sort at the interior of each of its images

                                                   and
so has art   a logic that connects these two images
autobiography and structuralism   because thats what they
are   images as theyve come to be understood in the world of
art   into two variations on a single theme which even has
a name   though not a very good one because its misleading
      but a popular one nonetheless   and thats "self
reference"   which ordinarily gets used in the art world to
characterize ostensibly structuralist works like the
sculpture of carl andre or mel bochner or sol lewitt   and
      occasionally robert morris or richard serra   but not
josef beuys or eva hesse or jackie winsor or jonathan
borofsky or italo scanga or eleanor antin   which would
  ⁃i suppose   count for most people in the art world as
autobiographical
                               and there is a sense in which this seems
   reasonable and obvious   as when youre looking at a film
like "la region centrale" by michael snow or a sculpture like
carl andres "lever"   which everyone knows is a sculpture
  about sculpture and a film about film   but how do they
know it
              because when we all know something it seems
permissible to ask how we know it   and the answer would be
quick in coming   theyre both self referential   but all
 things considered   that doesnt seem to answer the question
      because it doesnt tell us what aspect of "lever" tells
us it refers to itself   what aspect does the referring and
what part of its self does it refer to
                                            these questions may
   seem confusing but they may be clearer if i try to recall
the sculpture more precisely

              it was a work andre did back in 1966 for the
primary structures show   and it consisted of over a hundred
firebricks laid face to face forming a four inch high line
   that ran from the wall to the door through the middle of
one of those old fashioned wood panelled rooms of the jewish
museum

now what part of this scene that ive just recalled was
the work "lever"
a bunch of bricks laid face to face in a
straight line in an old fashioned room of a remodeled
mansion?   a bunch of bricks running in a straight line
through the middle of a room from wall to door?   or some
precise number of firebricks of some precise dimensions
139 bricks 2 1/2 x 4 1/2 x 8 7/8 inches   of some
particular mineral constituency arranged in a column on the
floor necessarily several feet below eye level?   or the act
of placing them there?

now suppose we say that most of the aspects of that
scene we've just called up   taken singly or together   are
reasonably likely to have constituted the whole work   the
self of "lever"   then we should be able to ask whether
any of these aspects of "lever" tells us that we should take
it or any other aspect as referring to itself or any other
aspect   or "lever" as a whole   and while this may not
seem a promising tack   one of these aspects   which may at
first seem the least promising   offers us a way to approach
this popular but elusive notion of self reference
"the act of
putting it there"   because "there" was not only a room in
the jewish museum   it was also a sculpture show   clearly
defined as sculpture by its curator   to the public in the
catalog and most likely to the artists who had been invited
so we could assume that any work included in the primary
structures show was being proposed   by the curator and
most likely the artist   as a candidate for consideration as
a work of sculpture   and while this isnt so much a mark
of the work as a marking of the context into which the work
was introduced   this is the site of whatever self
referencing action a work can perform
perform because a genre
is a theater defined by a history of the performances you
remember taking place within it   and any work seeking to
play that theater will be judged in relation to the history
of performance youve constructed for it
so the act of putting
it there   at least in part   means exercising a claim to

the right to be there   a right whose validity we can only
   judge by comparing aspects of this work to aspects of the
other works that have been there before it   at least when
the new work is sufficiently different to make its claim seem
questionable   or uncertain enough to propose the question
   of where "there" really is

                              yet even if you encountered
"lever" all by itself   in an art gallery or the artist's
   loft or the home of a collector   you would probably still
identify its arena as "sculpture"   a theater it shares
with a mark disuvero or a john chamberlain or a david smith
and a host of other works it only faintly resembles or the
henry moore outside this museum   which it doesnt resemble
at all   though you might not identify it so readily as
sculpture if you encountered it in an empty field or a school
playground or a city street   and a lot would depend on its
   placement there and whether it called to mind cleopatra's
needle or brancusi's endless column

                              as the response of many
of the natives of hartford to a more recent work of andre's
   which distributed a large number of locally quarried
boulders around the city square   suggests that a failure to
   bring to mind stonehenge or avebury was the main cause for
hostility from an audience who didnt think the work belonged
there   or more properly couldnt find in that place a
   "there" in which the work belonged

            now all art works make some kind of a generic
   claim   but some make it more and some less emphatically
      and some are so clearly like other works that everyone
knows have operated in some familiar theater that we
   recognize their claim so easily and quickly we're not aware
a claim has been made   and its only in the case of doubtful
   claimants that we're aware of a claim at all   though
doubtfulness will vary with the audiences experience and the
   artistic situation of the time   because only twelve or
thirteen years earlier works like andre's "lever" might have
   looked doubtful even to art world veterans like george
sugarman or mark disuvero and andre could have counted on
that for most of the works effect   while now he has to go
   outside the art world to the citizens of hartford to

   160

achieve even a roughly similar effect

roughly because making
a doubtful claim before the people of hartford would lead
predictably to quick dismissal   while making a doubtful
claim for the art world is to raise the first in a series of
questions that will establish what it thinks of as the
present avant-garde   and it is these questions   that
compare the arrangement and constitution and disposition of
this doubtful work with the arrangement constitution and
disposition of less doubtful and more familiar works   that
invoke the figure of self reference   which is a figure of
speech   as though "lever" simply in its being there should
declare   "look how simple i am   composed by sheer addition
of one and one and one   how low i am   how little space i
take   and how aggressively i take it   and how i'm not
balanced modified or fabricated   but simply chosen and
placed   yet do i not like all true sculpture 'articulate
the space?'"

in this talky form of self reference an art work
appears to compare itself to others

but what then?   if we
see its claim as just   is that all its going to do   if
we give you the keys to the theater arent you going to do a
performance there   or is the only performance the one
you do to get the keys?

it must have been some such questions
as these that many artists asked themselves around the
beginning of the 70s that led some of them to experiment with
that other form of self reference that we've been calling
"autobiography"

but maybe "autobiography" is not quite the
right word for what we mean by this sort of self referential
project because it suggests too much   the whole course of a
life   seen toward its end and summing up in its curve the
life of a great man   benjamin franklin   or lincoln
steffens   or the confessions of a saint   ancient like
augustine or modern like rousseau   or the memoirs of a
prince like kropotkin or a ballerina like karsavina   but
this is too much and theres nothing in the art world quite
like it   what we mean is something more like a diary a
journal or a notebook   or maybe only a few of its pages

or do we even mean that

if vito acconci each day takes one
object from his apartment near sheridan square to leave it
in a gallery on upper broadway   emptying in the course of
a conventional thirty day show his spare apartment of most
of the things on which his daily life depends   and he
finds himself riding the subway to make use of his table lamp
for reading or his kettle to brew himself a cup of tea
      do we   when we walk into the gallery and confront this
accumulation of used appliances and books and clothing feel
like we're reading a diary looking into an apartment or
witnessing a dispossession

i know that this jumble of things
has something to do with his life   it says so on the
gallery wall   but it has so little in common with the
purposeful sound of a diary   "i open this in order to say
that i had tea with dora at the club and was introduced to mr.
harold banks"   in spite of the kettle we dont even know
whether vito drinks tea or with whom or when or to what
purpose   and certainly not what he thinks of it or of them
or himself because nothing in this exhibition says "i" in the
manner of "finally i said goodbye to mathilde" or even "i
see for example the face of a friend"

still there may be other
ways of saying "i"   as there are other works that may say
it more clearly

for years italo scanga has been making a kind of
enigmatic sculpture that to most people suggested
autobiography devotional statues of saints painted over in a
casually gestural style and mounted at odd angles on
minimalist bases reframed kitsch icons accompanied by
mediterranean herbs like basil and oregano   giant heads
hacked out of wood and overpainted in a comic book cubism
each the site of some kind of collision between folk art
or the art of the folk and some kind of educated contemporary
art knowledge   which is explained   if at all   with
reference to scanga's well known calabrian origin   as though
an eleven or twelve or thirteen year old immigrant from the
italian south must be the persistent bearer of the tastes and
knowledges of a south italic cultural rubble that he is fated

162

to bring with him into every encounter with contemporary
american art   elio vittorini meet clement greenberg or don
judd or julian schnabel   and though you may not believe
this it is to scanga's artistic credit that he's the one who
has staged these encounters and told us how theyve gone in a
series of episodes   "CALABRIAN KID MEETS 'TRIUMPH OF
MODERN ART' CHOPS HEADS AND PAINTS CUBISM"
"CALABRIAN KID VISITS SOHO   LEAVES ICONS AND HERBS"
whatever you think of this work   it is clearly positioned for you to
always seem to hear it say "i"   or have no way to deal with it
at all

        but while we can locate in the sculpture of italo
scanga and the paintings of jonathan borofsky   or some of
the performances of vito acconci or adrian piper or eleanor
antin   a whole genre of such first person works   it is
still far from clear whether we are dealing with a theater of
fact or fiction
            after all gogol wrote "the diary of a madman"
    and italo svevo "the confessions of zeno"   and nobody
believes that zeno was svevo or gogol a madman   at least
not to the extent of identifying the "i" of the writer with
the "i" of the writing   and there are not many who will
    identify vito with the wild man in the basement   piper
with her "mythic being"   or antin with "antinova"
                                there is
something about autobiography that goes beyond the first
person discourse and lays claim to truth   which is a little
    bit more difficult to approach than the apparently
grammatical question of who it is that is talking   and
    maybe its a bit easier to approach this question in my own
    work   which is usually considered autobiographical and
makes a very definite claim to some kind of truth
                                now i'm a
performance poet or a language artist   and that may at
first seem quite different from a sculptor or painter or
filmmaker or video artist but i'm not so sure about that
    because working at language is a lot like working at
sculpture   theres a kind of stubborn material to it   the
language   thats only so ductile or tensile or strong   and
a poet doesnt create it   though it may seem that he does

but being a poet and working with language is a lot
like being a spider and working with silk because the
language comes out of your mouth much the way thread comes
out of a spider   so that it looks like youve made it   but
only in a way

          for as far as the silk goes   you havent got a
choice   the threads are made of exactly the same stuff for
each spider of your kind   and though you can choose to
bring them out singly or doubled or plaited into cable   the
choices are the same for all spiders of your family and
there are only a limited number of structures you can employ
for the web   whose elegant grammar belongs equally to all
of you   and while one poet spider may be more precise or
more casual in stretching the radii or unwinding a
logarithmic spiral of the chords   and this may be a matter
of personal acuity or taste   its still the same web
with the structural limitations of its type   like
english or french

          so the epeira has a sticky thread that the
labyrinth spider hasnt got   and the epeira family can lay
out a stark geometric web in a single plane perpendicular to
the ground   confident that a flying insect will stick
while the labyrinth spider has to lay out a three
dimensional maze to entangle insects in its web

          and like
spiders we poets are all beneficiaries and victims of our
language   there are limits to what we can do with it as we
move around in it   picking up the thread of a discourse
laying out others   adding adjusting and winding round
old ones   working always within the limits of the material
its constitution and character   according to our
habits and opportunities   our capabilities and needs   and
we ought to be able   i suppose   to distinguish one
spiders attitudes its style   from anothers the way we can
distinguish one american poet from another   not just an
american poet from a french one   if we have time enough or
care enough   by the way they adjust the character of their
web to the circumstances confronting them   and the values
they place on it   for i suppose spiders have values like
poets and artists

          but how should we assess the truth value

164

or truth claim   supposing it has one   of a web

should we
identify it with its functional effectiveness   by the
moths and the flies that it catches   however obviously this
 depends somewhat on circumstances and accident   or by the
spiders intensity of commitment to this function in spite of
 all accident   whose transparent representation we will
regard as a kind of truthfulness of the web   because it is
 stripped of all other apparent function than fly catching or
moth catching   the convention of naturalism

or we can
 imagine a commitment to a particular way of building that
has a value of its own   that the builder has to adjust
 tenaciously to his task of fly catching at great cost of
energy and time

somehow this sounds less likely   perhaps
because we're used to conventions of plausibility in
assessing the truth or truthfulness of biography and
 autobiography   as though we had an idea that we could tell
in advance what a fact should look like   or what would be
 the shape of a truly effective web

and then there is
 something about the motives as we feel them right now
underlying this autobiographical project in art   that tends
to support this taste for the plausible   a sense of the
commonness of our lives   rather than their singularity
   that connects the lives of artists with the lives of
everyone else   in their meanings and motives   and it is
as though this commonness of human concerns should provide a
 reason and basis for reading   that might replace the
common cultural mythologies of religion or nation or class
   which have eroded so long theyve seemed   from the
point of view of art   brittle armatures for two hundred
 years or more   and had already been replaced   for most
of us by a mythology of arts career   its well known
  history in progress and troubles   in which it sinks and
 rises like a hero of richard strauss   and is perhaps all
that lets us read or want to read a painting by rothko or
newman or brice marden

and while i sympathize with this taste and

motivation for the commonness of autobiography as the
commonness of our lives and our world   and to some extent
share it   i have a deep distrust of the plausible   and i
suspect that what we have most in common is the profound
singularity and implausible detail of our generally common
lives   and for that reason i want to tell you something of
the life of my friend nasi   the only true structuralist i
ever really knew   whose life was not particularly plausible
or common   but whose singularity was common to
structuralism and may reveal something about it that is
nevertheless fundamentally true

now i dont like to say this because it sounds
very colorful and implausible   but nasi was a red headed
dwarf whose real name was either athanasius or anastasius
and he was either polish or greek   i was never quite sure
because he spoke both languages fluently as he spoke
twenty-five or six other languages as well   most of the
ones i knew with a distinctive and curious accent i was never
able to place with any certainty between the aegean and the
baltic seas   he may as i once heard have been brought up
in kars among turkish speaking armenians by a polish mother
and a greek father   and this is all very colorful but a
lot of the color is in how you say it   because nasi   as
everyone called him   was either a tall dwarf or a very
short and muscular little person

the first time i met him was in the gym of the west
twenty-third street y   i was working for a publishing
company on twenty-third over by fourth avenue and i used to
come early in the morning to swim before going on to work
that morning i couldnt quite wake up in the water and i
walked into the gym to try working out on the mats when i saw
this little red bearded fellow rushing up the ropes his body
held neatly in an "L"   he did this several times
finished by dropping to the mat on which he did three
successive back flips followed by three forward flips clapped
his hands in satisfaction and started for the locker room
when i expressed my admiration he smiled and said "body
is image of god   needs daily polishing" and walked away
the next time i ran into nasi was in a translation
agency conference held some place in murray hill   it turned

out he was one of the people working for alexander gode
      translating scientific articles from a number of
european languages into interlingua   a kind of synthetic
pan romance language with a simplified grammar designed by a
bunch of linguists for international scientific communication
      gode was one of its inventors and president of the
interlingua institute   which he ran out of a greenwich
village office along with his translating agency   for which
nasi also translated technical articles mainly from czech
and polish and russian
                              he smiled when he saw me and came
across the room to shake my hand "yes" he said "david i
am linguist and poet   hence i am interested in all things
linguistic   even that vaporous monster interlingua   which
i am feeding all time now   in a previous life i was
ingenieur"

         strange as it seemed that i'd never met him before
      because we'd worked for most of the same seven or eight
companies that paid well and reliably enough to make it worth
our while reading german chemical patents russian physics
      monographs or french pharmaceutical texts   it was natural
enough because translation work is done almost entirely by
      freelancers   peculiarly skilled private people with some
personal reason for needing preferring and sometimes
delighting in the ebb and flow of this often randomly varying
      part time work carrying fragments of knowledge of belgian
mental hospitals azar fertilizer plants or swedish fish farms
      who most often had their own consuming private projects and
appeared in translation offices rarely and only   so it
      seemed   for some momentary contact with a world outside
themselves   with which they might exchange a joke or some
      comments about the   city or the weather   pick up or
return their packets and then be gone

         but once i met nasi it seemed that i ran into him
nearly everywhere   at a loft party for michael lekakis an
      elegant wood sculptor   who was having an opening i think
      i noticed nasi   accompanied by a beautiful dark haired
eurasian woman   standing beside a table pouring himself a
      glass of ouzo

                                                         167

"thats genya" my friend gene told me "and nasi
the painter"
        "genya?" i said "sounds polish"   gene shrugged
    "thats what he calls her   shes his model
theyre always together"

        later i found out that her name was really yen lü
    which nasi had converted over time into the more
familiar genya   and they made an odd couple together   nasi
 stocky and disheveled in wide waled old yellow corduroys
 laced-up work boots and cable knit sweater   his friend
tall and slim in short cut hair   pale makeup and dark nail
 polish   impeccably dressed in what looked like a thirties
tailored suit high heeled shoes and nylon stockings   and in
 their expressions too   nasi always mobile squinting
  screwing up his mouth and sneering or laughing   genya so
cool she seemed almost sullen   though usually polite when
 she wasnt ironic or lightly mocking   which she nearly
 always seemed to be when you got to know her   holding out
a cool hand to acquiesce to a greeting nodding faintly to
  acknowledge a joke or smiling with all the enthusiasm of a
hostess in a high class bar   and this was a style she could
 maintain even while dancing   no mean feat for someone
  dancing with nasi   who loved to dance and was a kind of
 percussive demon at any loft party where there was music
        and he would dance anything from greek and israeli
 circle dances to czardases and polkas   rhumbas and sambas
and mambos   even lindy hops with the same athletic furor
    in the midst of this storm genya would usually be moving
calmly always correctly but so slightly she seemed to be
 almost standing still   turning a hip   inflecting a
 shoulder inclining her head or just raising an eyebrow   to
 punctuate the melody or rhythm and somehow hold her own

            and this was a performance i saw many times because
 nasi loved to party the way he loved to drink   when i got
 to know him better we used to lunch together sometimes at a
 little german bakery on second avenue paul blackburn
 introduced us to   that didnt carry liquor but looked the
  other way if you brought your own   and nasi always seemed
    to bring his own   a flask of stolichnaya or some ouzo
 that he would fill up a water glass with and toss off neat

a trick i couldnt hope to match   but with liquor i
liked better than paul's sweet brandy   yet for all that he
drank i never saw nasi get smashed or any higher than he
usually was when sober   though maybe a little more emphatic
and oracular

the closest i ever saw him come to this was at a
literary party where there was no dancing but a lot to drink
it was over by gramercy park in a hall that belonged to
the national academy of arts and letters and was in honor of
the chelsea review   a literary magazine run by some
friends of mine that published a lot of european fiction and
poetry in translation and i had translated a martin buber
story from the german for their first issue   which as i
remember had just come out

so the place was filled with poets and novelists
literary people   translators editors and agents   and i
was talking with jerome rothenberg and george economou
when i caught a glimpse of george reavey the russian
translator   a waxy little handsome man talking   strangely
i thought to a child   he made a sort of sweeping gesture
with his arm   some kind of ironic disclaimer that turned
him half way around   and i realized he was talking to nasi
i figured they were having a linguistic argument
probably about translation and i walked over to hear

reavey had translated a book of mayakovsky and nasi
was berating him for it

"why do you not translate true poets   blok or
byely   or pioneers like kruchonykh or khlebnikov?
mayakovski is just a lackey who steals masters silver to
juggle in the streets   a buffoon a clown   pah   i spit
on mayakovski   turns poesy into pigsty for petit bourgeois
bolsheviki   makes tin pan alley jingles for tin ear
public   tunes for tax collectors   he is not fit to be
valet to carry saintly velimir upon his back   god bless his
rotten legs   it is not with such a one that poesy will ever
thrive   that sentimental mercenary bandit"

it was a long argument with reavey a little pompous
and ironic and nasi as always over violent and i didnt stay

to hear the whole thing   but long enough to hear reaveys
rejoinder about kruchonykh whose great success consisted of
emptying words of all their meaning   and nasi's response
that you cannot empty anything without filling it with
something else

       "when you empty a glass of water you fill it up
with air"
       and to ask nasi what did kruchonykh fill the
emptied words with?   and hear him answer

       "spirit"

       before i walked off to say hello to ursule
who was talking to a plump and rosy cheeked middle aged
german sounding guy   who wanted to know how the magazine
had come by its name and what was meant by it   fingering her
old fashioned garnet ring and smiling dryly ursule gave a
meticulous explanation   it had been a long afternoon at the
cafe cino and all sorts of names had come up   "trobar clus"
"chert" "greve"   joan kelly came up with "boars
head"   which sounded like an english tavern and venable and
ursule had an apartment in the west twenties   which the real
estate developers all called chelsea   that also sounded
english   and amused almost everyone   and that became
its name
       "so why then is the paper so bad" the german
demanded

       and i walked off to rejoin my other friends   who
were talking about something like magic wands and alistair
crowley   when george let out a soft cry of admiration and i
looked toward the door   through which a startling couple
were making a kind of grand entrance   a tall handsome young
woman in a full skirted summer dress under an immense brimmed
and ribbon bedecked southern belle hat   on the arm of a
tiny mouselike man in a formal suit over whom she towered
like some grand ocean liner drawn by a tug   "who's that?"
said george   "oscar williams" said venable   "no i mean
the girl"   but nobody knew though it turned to be rochelle
owens the poet and playwright who i suppose everybody knows
now   while who remembers oscar williams?

       though for anybody

who doesnt   he was a kind of a wretchedly mediocre poet
     one of a swarm living off the corpse of dylan thomas'
rhetoric   and a kind of modern day palgrave   whose real
 distinction seems to have been the ability to capture the
 imagination of american publishing with a succession of
little treasuries of verse   mini anthologies of modern
    poetry   modern american poetry immortal poetry   the
distinguishing features of which were tiny portraits of all
 of the poets and a system of selection according to which
    oscar williams and gene derwood outrepresented william
 carlos williams by a ratio of three to one

               on his way in oscar made a very roundabout tour of
     the room stopping to greet each editor and agent in turn on
his way to the drink table where nasi   to whom he nodded and
seemed to know   was still arguing with reavey an italian
 poet and a greek translator while working his way through a
  bottle of vodka that he held in his hand and waved in the
  air to punctuate points in his discourse   nasi as i later
learned didnt seem to change much when he got drunk   except
 that his usually reddish face would start to pale save where
his otherwise nearly invisible pock marks gave him a kind of
  mottled look   that was a danger sign which his friends paid
   attention to
                    williams had joined the conversation with harry
roskolenko   reavey had gone and rochelle had wandered off to
say hello to someone and was standing and talking with my
   friend george   the energy of the conversation had shifted
somewhat to roskolenko and williams   with nasi simply
watching   roskolenko seeming sort of sarcastic and
 aggressive and williams appearing a little disdainful and
  pompous while nasi kept drinking and watching through
  narrowed eyes   later i heard that roskolenko had been
  baiting oscar about giving up his good jewish name for a
commonplace goyish one   a charge to which williams responded
at first ironically   in the name of a kind of universalized
 religion that descended into a somewhat pedantic exposition
  of philosophical deism and ended with a clinching proof of
  the existence of god

          "if you found a watch in the street you would
  suppose it had a maker   so if you found a world in the

street . . ."   which was greeted by a roar of
        "BULLSHIT OSCAR"
                            from the italian poet   while nasi
leaped onto the table scattering bottles and glasses in all
directions and poured the remains of his vodka onto williams
  head

        when i asked him many months later why he had done
it nasi told me "i am linguist and christian   man is made
in image of god   to turn to idiot is sacrilege"   we were
sitting in the waldorf   one of those all night cafeterias
that used to shelter in their eerie yellow light a motley
group of sleepless city people who preferred to talk or sit
the night away in some kind of public company before
returning to their apartments lofts or furnished rooms
    this was a kind of grungy one on sixth avenue near the
8th street subway exit   and was a haven for years for street
people vagrants village intellectuals insomniacs till they
wrecked it in the sixties the way cities do to put up a soft
drink stand a notions store and then a bank
                                    but one day
returning from the bronx by the subway late   i learned i
could find nasi holding up one end of a discussion at the
waldorf most nights of the week   he came there mostly after
working at translation which he found an exhausting but
exhilarating labor

        "it is the language not the work that is
exhilarating" he told me   "so i come here to talk to calm
myself and drink some tea"   and where nasi sat drinking his
tea russian style with lemon and from a glass that he brought
to his mouth where he kept a half lump of sugar that he
sipped it through   was a kind of language circle to which
raffish scholars came to propose theories of the descent of
german from yiddish   why lip formed consonants were
missing from tlingit   or of the adequacy of a language
based entirely on the seven notes of the musical scale
    theories i learned to take more seriously in spite of
their extravagant appearance as i learned more about the
subject and the identity of the proponents

        nasi i found out was a formidably trained linguist

172

who had studied in warsaw and prague and had been a sort of
peripheral member of the linguistic circle of prague
    "i am structuralist and christian" nasi said
    "i understand the structuralist   nasi   but why
christian?"
    "because i am linguist and god is logos   which is
language"
    "but i'm also a linguist and i'm not a christian
it doesnt occur to me to be a christian"
    "yes but you are jew and forget that god is born
and dies in your mouth again every time you speak   and
there is no language without speech   without which god is
dead   you must study david   because it is all there in
baudouin and in troubetskoy   above all in troubetskoy
    you must study troubetskoy   it is all there in *les
principes de phonologie"*   and he said this to me many times
but i must admit i was somewhat puzzled by this because i was
not really familiar with baudouin de courtenay at that time
    i had read troubetskoys work on phonology several times
and had never noticed the slightest indication of
spirituality or religiosity in that rather elegant but
    somewhat positivist scientific work   and though he
commended it to me many times
                                      "les principes   les principes
david   it is all in *les principes"*
                                    i never understood
nasi's reading of prince troubetskoy till i had the
opportunity to see nasi's paintings   which happened one
morning after an all night session at the waldorf on
    universal languages   one of those rambling marathons
started by a handful of people around a table early in the
evening that would meander and spread to accommodate new
arrivals   who would drop in during the course of the night
    and listen for a while before picking up the thread of the
argument left hanging by the departures of others   leaving
by morning only a few veterans who had stayed the whole
course still talking
                  in this case mr. chao   a small balding
gentleman with a fringe of very dark hair   who always wore
the same shiny blue business suit and carried around a
childs old fashioned brown leather briefcase stuffed with the

chinese and japanese manuscripts that he was annotating or
translating for this or that institution or scholar   a
wolfish faced pale eyed serbian linguist named bogdan and
nasi

as i remember it all started out as a dispute over
the relative merits of esperanto and interlingua   which
found nasi somewhat perversely   because he worked for
interlingua   but not so surprisingly   since by then i
almost expected it of him   on the side of esperanto and
against interlingua

"its not a language   it is a code for translating
articles on cardiology" he had said   of the language he
translated into and out of and edited nearly every day
"so you are enlisting under the green flag nasi?"
said bogdan with a wink at me and mr. chao   that set nasi off
"your countryman lapenna wouldnt let me wear it
anyway   i'm too much of a crank for him"

dr. ivo lapenna was
a yugoslavian scholar and professor of international law at
the london school of economics   he'd been the leading
figure in the esperanto movement since the end of the second
world war   and green was the movement's traditional
symbolic color and was often worn by its more flamboyant
members   who would frequently show up at international
congresses decked out in loud green blazers or dresses and
bright green shoes or stockings   or adorned with yellow
neckties spangled with green stars or sporting green stars
on armbands and badges and sometimes carrying little green
flags or pennants as a sign of their devotion to the "inner
idea" of esperanto   which consisted of a cluster of sweet
beliefs in peace justice and brotherhood that would be
brought about through the mutual understanding fostered by
an international language

an idea that happened also to be
supported by the suave dr. lapenna   on whom the green
fashions acted somewhat like a red flag on a bull and drove
him to flights of furor against the movements "cranks and
eccentrics"   all of whom he regarded as so many obstacles
impeding the progress of his own sensible negotiations on
esperantos behalf with various national and international

174

agencies   like unesco
          which nasi took a dim view of   the
same dim view he took of dr. lapenna and most of the other
figures of the international language movement
           with the sole
exception of the "saintly founder" of esperanto   the polish
jewish oculist ludwig lazar zamenhof

    it was nasi's unexpected praise for zamenhof that
triggered the real argument   zamenhof the bialystok born
dr. esperanto the hopeful scholar ex-medical student ex-doctor
ex-zionist utopian linguist sweet humanist and impoverished
oculist who out of his experience of bialystok where four
religions and four languages divided in continual discord and
violence a population where orthodox russians ruled catholic
poles protestant prussians and a large number of jews   had
devised from pieces of french and latin and german and polish
and russian a simple and easy to learn international language
to bridge the gulf between nations and heal the wounds among
peoples
        which with the help of a mr. zilbernik   his
businessman father-in-law   he presented to the russian
polish german and french speaking worlds in 1888

        bogdan   who had been laughing out of his pale
slanted eyes while nasi was speaking started singing in a low
voice almost under his breath
      "malamikete de las nacjes   kado! kado! jam temp
esta   lat tot homoze en familje komunigare so deba"
    "and is it not one human family" nasi protested "it
is one because language is one and god is one and human mind is
one and that is almost the same thing"
    "admit it nasi   it was a mistake   a mistake
founded on a mistake"   our serbian friend had charged
    laughing out of his pale slanted eyes   "a mistake so
great it took a philosopher to make it"

    that started a discussion of descartes because
according to bogdan   it was all in descartes   and there
wasnt a single idea good or bad for an international language
    whether it was a real vernacular or an international
trade language or a universal scientific language   that

couldnt be found in two paragraphs of descartes letter to
mersenne

       mr. chao was not convinced   he objected that
there was a world of difference between the abstract
language projects of philosophers and mathematicians like
  descartes and leibnitz or even scientists like dalgarno and
wilkins   and practical and serious projects for an
  international language like volapük or esperanto   which
were designed for use by everyone were modeled on existing
languages but were so regular that with a little effort they
could be learned by anyone

                           but for bogdan it all boiled down
to the same thing   the two virtues   regularity and
simplicity   simplicity and regularity   which were like
 the two faces of a single coin   because you could roll
them over and over again and they would mark the same metal
   simplicity and regularity of thinking for the scientific
languages   regularity and simplicity of expression for our
vernaculars   because at the center was this idea that our
existing languages were not clear enough   for thinking or
expressing   because they were not simple enough or regular
enough   and had probably been corrupted by centuries of
usage from whatever logical clarity they had once possessed
   which we could restore and improve upon if we could only
design them all over again to be simpler and more regular
than any language we had ever known

                        which we could easily do
because all we would have to do would be to set up the rules
 of the grammar so that there were very few of them   make
sure that they would all apply regularly and without
exception in all instances and cases

     we would make all noun declensions one declension
all of their cases one case   their genders one gender
eliminating the differences between singulars and plurals the
same way we got rid of the duals who needs them anyway as
long as youve got numbers   we would do the same for the
verbs   collapsing all conjugations into one conjugation
all persons into one person   we've got pronouns havent we
   and then we could get rid of the tenses because we've
got adverbs like "now" or "then" or "earlier" or "later" or

176

"yesterday" or "tomorrow" or "the middle of next week"   and
similarly we could get rid of the modes because we could
always say "maybe" "probably" "possibly" or "hopefully"
"wishfully" or "isnt that so"   and after a while we would
end up with a language that any salesman or school child
could learn on a bus trip or a plane ride

while for the philosophically minded or the
scientific or political   all we would need to add to this
would be a complete list of all the basic ideas that have
ever occurred to the human mind along with a list of rules
for combining them into all of the new and complex ideas that
might ever occur in the future   maybe together with some
system of spelling that would give a clear and unambiguous
picture of where these complex ideas had come from   this
whole system would be so simple that it could make a
scientist out of a plumber a philosopher out of the
salesman and a statesman out of a boy scout because it would
enable them to evaluate serious scientific philosophical and
ethical problems in less time than a professor now struggling
in chinese or russian or french

"its a wonderful idea" said bogdan who had been
playing all this time idly with the silverware left on the
table over the course of the evening by all of the visitors
who had come and gone   and by now had built a remarkable
leaning structure several feet high with a scaffolding of
forks and spoons and knives balancing platforms of saucers
and dishes capped by teacups for domes

"and it is always the same idea   all of these
workers working skillfully and harmoniously to build a tall
and beautiful tower   and working so long and so hard that
the workers at the top begin to sleep and eat at the top
while the workers at the bottom begin to live at the
bottom   so that the workers at the top only speak to the
other workers at the top and they forget how to speak to
the workers at the bottom   and the workers at the bottom
forget how to understand the workers at the top   till
nobody can understand anyone elses instructions and they all
start to fight one with another about how the building of
the tower should go   and this one says this and that one

says that   but nobody understands anybody who works in a
   different part of the tower   and they all get so mad with
each other that they destroy the building and most of each
other out of spite except for one or two survivors maybe
engineers   who decide they could all work it out and build
up the tower again   but only after they work out a
language so simple and so clear that everyone can learn it
   and no one can forget it"

                            at this point he started to take
all of the dishes and saucers and spoons and knives out of
   his building   reducing it to a small and crooked
structure built entirely out of forks   which he struck
lightly with his hand and watched totter and fall

        "its ridiculous"

        mr. chao was still not convinced   it was of
course charming to say so and even in some part true   for
as most of our distinguished colleagues no doubt knew   that
   gentle optician the same who founded esperanto   the
blessed ludwig lazar zamenhof   and with this mr. chao looked
at nasi   had written in his early youth a five act tragedy
   on the theme of the celebrated fallen tower   and nasi
nodded

        "and yet" mr. chao went on "that is not quite the
whole story   for the two great invented international
   languages   leaving aside the communally constructed
linguae francae like the oceanic pigeons or malay or swahili
or even yiddish or vulgar latin or the greek koine   the
   two invented international languages that have had grand
success could be said to have flourished and attained
perhaps a million speakers   volapük and esperanto were
not especially simple   though they were quite regular and
easy enough to learn

                        for as you no doubt know volapük had
four cases for the noun a verb system modeled on ancient
greek with six tenses and six modes   including distinct
imperative jussive optative and subjunctive forms that could
be employed in all six tenses   as indeed could the
infinitive   this was not simple and volapük had been
   much blamed for this   and with some justice   by the

178

american philosophical society among others   while
esperanto though much simpler in grammatical forms had an
accusative case and an unusual plural and required adjective
noun concord in the accusative singular and plural   as well
as a complex system of derivational affixes   all of which
had been criticized by linguistic scientists   yet
    notwithstanding   it thrives   or at least survives as
volapük might also have survived   and not because but in
spite of what one might call the   fetish and bugaboo of all
philosophical and a priori languages   simplicity

        no it was not simplicity   not grammatical
simplicity nor conceptual simplicity that the parish priest
of litzelstetten dreamt of on that sleepless night of 1879
    it was of peace and the brotherhood of man   and
because father schleyer was a musician and a poet   and
above all a linguist   he thought to achieve this
brotherhood through a new and universal language for all
inhabitants of the earth   that he sought to design out
of the most useful parts of the more than fifty old ones
he was reputed to have known   which as was their habit
expressed national rather than human unity   by all the
affective means at their disposal

        mr. chao's father had been a delegate from tientsin
to the great volapük congress of paris of 1889 and it was an
    occasion he would never forget   he had been chosen by a
competition as the mission schools most fluent speaker of
volapük   in which he delivered a two hour oration on the
unity of gods creation   the judges were the instructors
    with whom he debated also in volapük   on the theme
that to render unto caeser was to create a human imperium
under god   his trip to paris was financed by a
subscription taken up by the british missionary society and
he arrived in paris in august   to find nearly two hundred
other volapükists from all over the world gathered to
    converse in volapük and come to some kind of agreement on
various nice points of volapük grammar   that some of the
more prestigious delegates had projects for simplifying

        but for mr. chao's father it was enough to be young
in paris on his own   taking in the sights and essaying

                                        179

his lingistic powers in the new language   which seemed to
  be spoken everywhere   in trams and department stores
      one of the great department stores   *printemps*   had
even given courses in the new language   so that while he
  dutifully attended most of the general sessions of the
  congress and intermittently followed the intricate debates
of the rules committee   marvelling at the subtlety of the
  members of the great council and the academicians   the
kademals and kademels   and the wondrous and learned
  proficiency of monsieur le professeur auguste kerckhoffs
    and the eloquence verging on genius of the cefal and
inventor of volapük msgr. schleyer   mr. chao's father spent
  most of his time cheerfully conversing with fellow delegates
and chiefly with another chinese delegate   a professional man
from canton who had brought his family along   his wife and
  charming daughter   who was studying western nursing and
was also an adept of volapük

        and it was with this young and attractive daughter
that mr. chao spent most of his time in paris   and because
  this was the summer of 1889   just one hundred years from
the beginning of the french revolution   this summer paris
    was host to a great international fair celebrating the
  products of enlightenment   technical progress and
commercial expansion   so the young couple spent most of
  their time strolling not only through the tuileries and
  the jardin des plantes or sailing in bateaux mouches up and
down the seine   but riding the little exposition trains
  that ran in a small circle from the esplanade des invalides
    with its javanese temples and cairo streets   complete
with bazaars and beggars   to the grand entrance at the
  champ de mars of the palace of machines into which they
  entered on foot and strolled under the overhead travelling
car and the sweltering heat of the vast glass and iron shed
    through the racketing industry of hundreds of twirling
  spinning pumping and reciprocating engines amid which they
    inspected harvesters compound locomotives tested
typewriters and listened through little earphones to people
speaking on edison's phonograph   but above all they visited
  and revisited and marvelled at by day and by night the
tallest building in the world   the three hundred meter

tower that eiffel had just completed in time for the
opening of the exposition   of which it was considered the
crowning jewel illuminated by thousands of electric light
bulbs and upon which it played nightly its red white and
blue beacon light   climbing to the first and second
landings to map out paris below them in the daylight or to
watch the fireworks fall nightly over the seine

but since mr.
chao's father came from tientsin in the north   where they
spoke a mandarin dialect of chinese with only four tones
and the young lady from distant canton in the south
where they spoke a quite different dialect of chinese
with nine   all of the conversations of the young couple
that had to surpass the meager resources of their pigeon
french or their few common words of chinese had to be
conducted in their new language   volapük

so that when they
ascended to the third and topmost landing of the tower
finally   just one hour before dusk   breathless and
flushed from the climb   and regarded the country that
stretched below them all the way to compiegne   when they
clasped their hands together they had to murmur shyly the
unaccustomed words   *loefebs okis*   which in volapük
means   "we love each other"

so it happened that mr. chao's father and the young
lady who became his mother failed to notice the terrible if
concealed struggle between professor kerckhoffs and msgr.
schleyer over the fate of the language in which their union
was sealed   terrible because it was concealed even from
these two leaders of the volapük movement   who were not
enemies in the true sense of the word   for as the two
prime advocates of volapük professor kerckhoffs and msgr.
schleyer simply stood on opposite sides of the same language
they offered the world as a medium of international
communication for all people

msgr. schleyer   the inventor   poet priest and
musician   had dreamt of a single unifying language whose
poetic power and intellectual beauty would be great enough
to express every shade of human meaning and satisfy every
human need for communication by creating a common language

181

reservoir vast enough to unite the tributary flow of the
huge fragmentary holdings of thought and feeling and
experience gathered up so partially in the different memories
 of our native tongues

      kerckhoffs was a businessman   a professor of
modern languages in a business institute who saw the
possibilities of schleyer's invention for science commerce
 and tourism   as a kind of international shorthand useful
in stock exchanges trade conferences laboratories and courts
of law   he had arranged for the third international
volapük congress to coincide with the paris world fair
   to draw an international attendance   where the
 earlier conferences at friederichshafen and munich had
mainly attracted a german attendance   he had also
 prepared for this by arranging courses in volapük to be
given free of charge in department stores and technical
 institutes all over paris   and in turin and reggio
d'emilia as well   he was the founder of the french
 association for the propagation of volapük   which he had
adorned with a central committee staffed by a string of
french notables

      kerckhoffs had personally edited a french teaching
text of volapük an abridged grammar of volapük a french
volapük dictionary and a complete volapük grammar

                           and where
msgr. schleyer was concerned with writing and translating
 poetry into volapük   which he published regularly in his
volapüksbled   kerckhoffs was concerned with attracting
 new recruits to volapük and spreading the use of it across
europe   and he was most concerned with simplifying the
task of learning it to make it more accessible to larger
 numbers of people   so he had plans for pruning away the
luxuriant growths of the verbal system   stripping away the
unnecessary optative and jussive   restricting the six
 tenses of the conditional to two   suppressing declension
of the infinitive and its personal endings   rationalizing
the system of derivational affixes and the rules for word
compounding   and clearing away most of the abundant
 grammatical devices that he considered redundant irrational
retrograde   and obstacles to the acquisition and spread of

volapük

to achieve these purposes he had organized a volapük
academy   an executive and legislative body with authority
to oversee what he called normalization of the grammar   by
which professor kerckhoffs meant a radical simplification
    but which he represented as a mere housecleaning job
that would eliminate redundancies and straighten out
inconsistencies   and for this purpose kerckhoffs got
himself elected director of this body   with responsibility
for proposing the simplifications that he had created this
body with the power to approve or reject

    this was an arrangement that msgr. schleyer did not
approve   or straightforwardly oppose   for schleyer
volapük was already a living language with over a million
speakers who used the language everyday   he was its creator
and it was his child   and every change except the most
minor seemed to him like surgery on a living being that might
    disfigure some aspect of its expressive power   and though
as lifetime cefal of the volapük academy he possessed three
votes to everyone elses one   schleyer insisted on a veto
power over any proposed changes that he considered
    detrimental to the life of the language

    this brought msgr. schleyer into direct conflict
with the academy and with kerckhoffs because the veto power
contradicted the rules that had been formulated by the
previous volapük congresses which had created the roles of
    the academy the director and the cefal himself   but
schleyer refused to acknowledge that he was bound by
previous decisions in any way and he threatened to depose
    the director and replace him if he didnt get the veto in
spite of the constitution the academy the director and the
    three international congresses
                                    and while this quarrel was a
source of great embarrassment and irritation to professor
kerckhoffs and the academicians   most of it took place
    behind the scenes of the paris congress largely unnoticed by
    the regular delegates   most of whom went home cheered with
the experience of speaking and hearing volapük   which
    constituted the success of the congress   symbolized for

183

them by the small bronze replicas of eiffels tower   like
the one mr. chao still remembered on the mantelpiece of his
fathers home

but it wasnt long after the paris congress that the
struggle between kerckhoffs and the party of the volapük
reformists   and msgr. schleyer and the volapük
traditionalists came out into the open and soon afterward
    tore the little language community apart   only a few of
kerckhoffs reforms were accepted by the academy   he
resigned and was replaced by a more moderate reformist   a
    mr. rosenberger of st. petersberg   whom msgr. schleyer also
rejected   along with the acts of the congress the authority
of the academy and the director   and set up a new academy
that accepted his final authority

within a few years the linguistic community of
volapük had shrunk from an estimated million speakers to a
few hundred   who have by now almost all disappeared   and
volapük has to all intents and purposes passed from a living
language to a dead one

so mr. chao pointed out   volapük   as a
complicated language in respect of whose complexities and
illogicisms most of professor kerckhoffs criticisms were
valid   had been quite successful   while it was professor
kerckhoffs attempts to simplify and rationalize it that had
killed it   so that volapük is now known   if it is known
at all   only as a predecessor of esperanto   which nearly
encountered the same fate just a few years afterwards   even
    though dr. zamenhof had the benefit of volapüks prior
cautionary example

mr. chao's conclusion led to an elaborate argument
about the measurement of simplicity itself   which in
most of these discussions is based on counting   the
number of grammatical rules   of tenses declensions
affixes   but as someone pointed out   and i think it was
bogdan   there are two overlapping but really quite
distinct ideas of simplicity that are always trotted out for
    the evaluation of synthetic languages   one is a kind of
occam's razor forbidding a superfluity of means   there
shall not be two grammatical forms to mark one distinction

or any grammatical form to mark an unnecessary one   in this
sense hungarian is simpler than english in its pronouns
because where english distinguishes "he" and "she" in the
third person singular the magyar simply says "oe"   and the
english past tense   which has the same form for all
persons numbers and genders   is simpler than the russian
which is inflected for both gender and number

but there is another sense in which simpler means
less difficult   to learn   to teach   to pronounce or to
distinguish   and about this we know next to nothing   yet
its easy to decide that the more rules a language has the
harder it is to learn   and this may seem obvious from our
experience in schools   where languages are taught by rules
and dead languages like latin and greek have lots of
rules and seem hard to learn because of them   but nobody
has ever been able to count all the rules of a living natural
language to compare it to another   and its not so obvious
why when people try to learn english   which seems to have
very few rules   it turns out to be so hard to learn that
very few foreigners ever learn to speak it correctly   which
people say is a question of usage   but then there are the
rules of usage   and nobody has ever counted them

so it may be that english has a great many rules of
usage   many more than ancient greek   because greek is a
dead language that nobody really uses   and so nobody laughs
at us for our mistakes of usage when we misuse it   but as
it stands the rules of english must be more numerous than
greek or sanskrit   and theyre even more difficult to
express   which is less a fact of these languages than of
our relative distances from them   which leads to bogdans
hypothesis that i offer in my version

no language is any simpler or any more complicated
than any other   they merely have their complications in
different places   and this is true for all natural
languages   which are social constructs that have evolved
among people   which are different from invented languages
made up for any purpose   whose real difficulties nobody can
really assess   because nobody knows the intelligibility
requirements of the human mind or what or how much it can or

cannot process efficiently poorly or at all   so that a
synthetic language might contain any number of difficulties
 or even impossibilities of perception articulation and
expression and nobody would know it   because we have only
the vaguest notions of what these are   but   and to this
let me add bogdan's first corollary these difficulties would
all be ironed out once people had really begun to speak this
 language and use it for all the different purposes of a
real language   if they continued to use it for a long
enough period of time   though nobody knows how long this
is   so bogdan

            now nasi   who had been silent for a long time and
sat quietly through many glasses of iced tea and had now
switched over to jello and seemed to agree   started to tap
his jello glass very excitedly and began to take the little
green red and yellow cubes out of the sundae cup and lay
them out on a napkin in patterns of twos and threes and
fours

            "what you are saying you are right   the mind of
man delights in the intricacies and difficulties of the
grammar he has invented   because he had invented it   not
personally of course   but socially and communally through
history as a people   through reflection and speculation on
objects actions states and processes   existences
nonexistences   possibilities   impossibilities   and
virtualities of all sorts
            every natural language is a junkyard of
philosophizing   which is its grammar   the cases of the
noun and the aspects of the verb   or the sentence order is
a peoples physics   sometimes ethics   the voices of the
verb are sometimes physics sometimes epistemology   while
the modes are sometimes epistemology and sometimes metaphysics
            this is why all the languages are complicated and
different   and this is why languages are delightful to
think about and a pleasure to talk about   but this is
languages   which man has invented and we are always talking
 about   not language   which is from god and we dont know
how to talk about it yet
            because language is one   as god is one   is
therefore too simple to take hold of and too hard   *en*

arkhei eyn ho logos   in the beginning was language   this
is maybe simple because the logos   that is *la langue*
     which is language   but   *kai ho logos eyn pros ton*
theon   and language was to god   that is hard   because
what must be god that language is to god or with god?
     because language also is god   *kai theos eyn ho logos*
     which is a mystery that i try to understand in the
following way
               logos   that is *la langue*   that is the rational
order what makes all signification possible   that is *la*
langue   which is god   but what then is god apart from
language?   god is what has created everything that has been
  created and without which not one single thing was created
     and this is what means   *in god all that has been*
created has been stirred into life and this life was the
light of the world   which is a dark saying till i interpret
 as follows
               god is *la langue*   but is more than the logical
order of mind   god is also the will to speak   the wind
that blows the breath of life into the logical order   is
the *ruakh* or *pneuma* that can blow all the logical order of
la langue to chaos   which is by its name a gas   but is
also the breath of life and the will to creation and to
 speech   which always threatens the order
               so this is the two things   the *logos* that is *la*
langue and god   and the breath that is the wind   which is
 the will that is also god   and that leaves only one to get
three   didnt i tell you i was christian?   and all that is
 missing then is the third thing   which is the body   and
 sure enough   the *langue* was made flesh   *ho logos sarks*
egeneto
               because the logical order and the will to speak is not
 yet enough   there needs yet the world and its limits
     needs mankind and body and mouth   needs lips and
 tongue and teeth   gums and palate   velum uvula the
 glottis and the caves of the nasal passage and the pharynx to
 set limits to spirit   to squeeze rub knead roll crush and
  contain the godly breath   with spit and phlegm and mucus
     to make something solid out of the air that is also the
 will and light   which is *la parole*   that is the third
 part of the trinity that is language"

and saying this he
pointed to the little cubes of yellow green and orange jello
he had arranged in twos and threes on his napkin and added

"but all of this is before syntax   that is mans
creation   the truth of language   what makes it possible
and also the same all over the world must be more universal
and more simple
                    i say this as i am christian and
structuralist   and this simple and universal is in the
phonology as troubetzkoy has shown us in *les principes*
the basis of language is in the sounds and only the
sounds   these few sounds that from the combination of which
all over the earth we get all of the words and morphemes of
the languages of the world
                            why these sounds and no others?"
he pointed to his little cubes of jello   "because
there is sustenance in them   in these phonemes   though
where   is the mystery i am studying right now"

but it was a mystery he refused to explain until i
had seen his paintings   so we went off to look at them
early that morning after a last cup of coffee   taking a
bus up sixth avenue through the nearly empty streets of the
west village across fourteenth and up into the west 20s

nasis studio was on the top floor of an old factory
building between 7th and 8th over a buttonhole maker some
furriers and a ladies hatmaking outfit   and it looked like
an ordinary loft space until you went past the customary
safety locked and bolted steel door through a small
antechamber that served as a kind of cloakroom and passed
through a second white painted sliding steel door into the
main room   which like most artists lofts was tall and
airy with high windows that ran the length of both the walls
which must have formed the front and back of the building
but there the resemblance stopped because each of these
windows was covered with dark heavy velvet drapes   the
entire floor was covered with black and white tiles and in
the middle of the room flanked by two small palm trees was
a fountain that played into a sculpted stone basin in which
large goldfish swam

188

"it was a present from a friend   a stone
sculptor" he said   "from the old country"   when he saw my
look of surprise

what old country? i wondered   because the space
with the palm trees and tiles and oriental rugs rattan chairs
and dark inlaid wooden chests and tables and the heavily
carved fountain apparently combined the decorative resources
of greece albania bulgaria turkey and most of the middle
east   and some of the far east i thought when yen lü came
through a beaded curtain in a heavily brocaded black silk
kimono to see what we were up to

"i am showing david the paintings" nasi explained
and yen lü didnt seem any more surprised than she ever
did even though it was not yet six in the morning   just
nodded sleepily and disappeared back into the room she had
come from

thats when i noticed the paintings   there were
not very many of them hanging   five or six   and they
were small   by contemporary standards   the smallest was
not much over a foot in length and the largest not more than
three feet in the longest dimension   and they were all
rectangular and seemed to be in the same proportion   later
i learned this was quite precise   because nasi employed
only three sizes   8 by 13   13 by 21   and 21 by 34
and this meant something to him because of the numbers
which were based as he subsequently told me on the
golden section   in which the ratio of the width to the
length was equal to the ratio of the length to the sum of
the two

but it was not the proportions that struck me   it
was the style and the content of the paintings   if one
could call it that   they were oils done in what at first
looked like a very old fashioned manner   in a dream of
the manner of some queer renaissance master like piero di
cosimo   very precisely underpainted   probably on a
sanded gesso ground with many layers of glazes that trapped
and reflected light in a strange way which cast a pearly
bluish grey tone over the whole surface of the painting   or
rather immersed and bathed it in a translucent and yet

faintly opalescent fluid medium

  and then the paintings were all of the same subject
a woman in a 1930s looking dark suit with a white
blouse and high heels doing ordinary things walking up
and down stairs putting on gloves adjusting her hair
 straightening a stocking looking at her nails
 turning waiting or simply regarding another image
of herself performing some similar action in another plane a
microtone layer deeper or shallower in perspective from
whom she was completely separated as by a minute gap in the
paintings space and this second one regarding or ignoring
the first or considering a third identically dressed who
was performing the same vernacular actions in a place
several angstroms deeper or shallower and separated by the
same strangely gapped space every painting had five or six
of these women and they were all yen lü

  nasi led me to a wooden closet covered by a baluchi
rug and pulled it back to reveal a set of racks holding
several dozen more paintings he took them out and showed
them to me one by one and while they were all different in
detail in the number of planes and figures and their
 actions and their attitudes they were all the same in
their queer lighting and their strange space

  it wasnt till then that i noticed the large studio
easel in the far corner of the room with a painting on it
still in progress and a clothes tree next to it with the
dark 1930s woman's suit hanging from it and the pair of
dark red high heeled shoes stationed neatly beneath it

  nasi hastened over and turned the easel to face the
wall "excuse me david but it is not finished and i do
not like to show it because until it is finished it is
not even nothing it is less than nothing" he apologized
while i studied the other paintings

  "do you see what i mean" he said they are
structuralist paintings" he went to a samovar to get us
some tea

  "nasi" i said "theyre wonderful paintings" and
they were wonderful in their quaint mixture of modernity

190

and old fashionedness   in the delicacy of the drawing that
articulated even in this small scale striking particulars of
feature and stance without the pedantic detail of
precisionist realism or the self conscious brush strokes of
painters like soyer or marsh   "theyre wonderful paintings
    but what makes them structuralist nasi?"

        he had poured us some tea and drawn up two chairs
around a moroccan table   and sucking on his sugar cube
and sipping at his tea he said   "they articulate the
distinctive features of the medium"

        "and what are they?"

        "look at these paintings david   what you see?
    illusion?   out of collagenous colloidal substance that is
paint and cloth surface of the canvas comes illusion of space
    and light"   he poked a finger against the surface of the
painting he had picked up from the floor

        "this is illusion   but is illusion revealed as
    illusion   you look you see through to depths   but you
touch   is all surface and is gone   you see within because
    is all light and air and space   which when you touch is
hard like wood or stone   this is miracle that is illusion
        which remains illusion
                            this is what means self
referential structuralist painting   this is illusion that
    remains an illusion and a mystery   how out of these
    substances of paint and canvas comes air and space and
light   and this is likewise the way with language   because
    out of these sounds comes words and meanings and mind   and
then is the mystery   how come?
                            how come from the simple
    phoneme   which phonology has taught us is the meaningless
sound class that has only distinction of being different from
    all the other intrinsically meaningless but absolutely
different sound classes which make up the phonemes of a
    language we get all of the words that contain all of the
meanings of the language?

        how should we come by the meaningless differences
    between /tsh/ and /p/ from 'chalice' to 'palace'   or

between /i/ and /ey/ from 'reason' to 'raisin'   it is not
   possible for language to be born so   to come from the
   meaningless to the meaningful   is that not obvious?"

           and i had to admit that it was   but linguistics
had long ago abdicated its rights of inquiry into the origins
of language   which had been part of its own origin
        yet when it was put this way as nasi put it   couched
in contemporary phonologic theory   it seemed somehow
reasonable to ask some of the old questions once again   and
it was in modern terms that he put the whole argument
    which went something like this

           given the great achievements of universal phonetics
        that show how small a stock of sound classes are
employed to generate all the languages of the earth   and how these
appear to be subject to the same precise laws that enable or
annul their contrasts   it must appear evident that all
languages on the phonologic evidence derive from a single
source and that language was born only once on earth
                                          this was
   evident from phonology and only obscured by considerations
of syntax and grammar   which are comparatively trivial
and subject to reflection and fashion   and not in the same
sense fundamental to language but secondary developments
   as roman jakobson had surely intended to indicate by
titling his most profound work   which was dedicated to
phonology   "the fundamentals of language"
                                      the primacy of
   phonology was recognized everywhere and its achievements
were universally considered the great intellectual
contribution of true structuralism
                              and yet it did not go far
   enough   in its questions and hypotheses   and this was
because it had been confused with the obscuring and
   unscientific fashions of empiricism and positivism   but
the facts speak for themselves   the organization of the
   sound structures of all languages   deeply understood   is
      the same   so that language is one   that is proved

           but how could the purely arbitrary and meaningless
   phonemes give rise to morphemes and words   what could have

192

promoted the formation of the conventions that defined them
and stipulated their use as signs

imagine a congregation of
speechless animals proposing
"let /p/ /t/ and /k/ /f/ /r/ /b/
/d/ /g/ and /v/ with /i/ /e/ /a/ /o/ and /u/ in their
constellations signify everything we think about"

this is
the ridiculous form of our idea of the arbitrary phonemic
convention   and it is as impossible to imagine that
speech sounds were originally arbitrary as to imagine that
our present speech sounds are systematically symbolic
because it isnt possible to conceive how human animals
could have come to connect three or four dozen purely
arbitrary sound types with a proliferating world of real or
mental objects   and if they ever did   how they could have
remembered the connections once they had been made

so according to nasi we had to consider that the
phonemes of the worlds languages had to have undergone many
significant changes to become the arbitrary signifiers we
now know   and this was shown by all the great works on
historical linguistics of the last century   how the
continuing change in the sounds of genetically related
languages was always transforming words and morphemes and
driving them further and further away from each other to the
point of unrecognizability and unintelligibility
revealing how in several hundred years a common latin
had split into the mutually unintelligible languages of
italian romanian french spanish and portuguese   and in less
than two thousand indo european had divided into twelve
separate families stretching from india and persia to iceland
and the irish sea   so how much greater changes must we
suppose in the seventy thousand years that separate us
from our aurignacian ancestors who had a rich enough
culture   even art   for us to suppose they had already
received the gift of language in its fullest and richest
form

no   language the ursprache must have come even
earlier than to those gifted artisans and artists of the
european caves   more than one hundred thousand years ago

193

to the neanderthalers with their mastery of fire and their
careful burial practices   and probably even earlier to
the comrades of heidelberg man   who was on the same level
as peking man and java man   because language must have
come to man as soon as he became man   because it was
language that must have made him man   and so it had to
have come before the race divided   maybe half a million
years ago

        because it could only have come once   unnoted
and unobservable by us   because it had to begin more poorly
and more physically in associations of our sounds and sound
making with the objects of our attention and desire   and
these satisfying magical sounds that we could make and
remake at will must have been able to call to mind those
thousands of things and feelings   those fears and wishes
and dreams in the absence of their objects for the language   ,
connection to be made

        and even if these cries murmurs and shouts had no
intrinsic connection to the images they called up they surely
had to be capable of becoming associated with them through
repetition in the long glacial night   perhaps through the
long and close relation of nursing children with their
mothers   and in the close associations forced upon us by
the rigors of the pleistocene   but however this may have
been   it is only imaginable that originally there was some
fundamental representational if abstract connection   some
kind of affinity or affective glue that could link these
processes of the throat and mouth to the meanings they came
to signify   which line of reasoning   according to nasi
brought him to his most important discovery   "the
submorphemic sememe"

        here nasi explained to me how since the fundamental
linkage between sound and meaning could not be found in the
phoneme or in the morpheme itself   he had come to realize
that it had to reside in certain affectively suggestive
phoneme combinations   out of which the original words of
the ursprache must have been built   and how it was out of
these suggestively meaningful phoneme clusters   not out of
phonemes which were mere artifacts of contrastive analysis

194

that the words of our original language were made

but i had to interrupt because all my education and
training revolted at the notion of semantically significant
phoneme clusters

"come on nasi" i said   "surely you dont mean that
definite meanings attach to the sounds of words   how could
you explain that 'horse' and 'cheval' mean the same thing in
english and french and have no sounds in common?"

nasi shook his head   "thats too easy my friend
you are not really thinking   you are only reciting
what a whole generation of serious linguists before you have
also said without thinking   because you should know that
'horse' and 'cheval' dont mean same thing just because you
can sometimes translate one for other   a 'cheval' can be
ridden by 'chevalier'   who is already 'chivalric'   and a
'horse'"   said nasi   "is   if you will forgive me   an
animal of a different color

because if noblewoman wants to ride horse she is
probably 'equestrienne'   not 'horsewoman'   for the
'horse' has lost much of its color since it separates from
old germanic 'hros' or old norse 'hross'   where you can
still hear beats of his hooves   as in modern german 'rosse
getrabe'   which in that language plays more the role of
'steed' or 'courser' than plays the 'horse'   for which
german has the plainer word 'pferd'   which i consider is
more 'ploughhorse' or 'plug' than is even the 'horse'

"every way of pronouncing   every phonic
expression that gives shape to a word has possibility to be
different way of thinking and seeing   is different aspect
i dont want to say   of reality because that is too
vulgar   but of mental object
"so latin 'equus' and greek 'hippos' are two
different ways of thinking about the ungulate   but
'ungulate'   this is a biological way of thinking   an
abstraction like phoneme   which is linguistic abstraction
while russian 'loshad' and polish 'loszak' is the way of
thinking of little tartar horse   and 'kon'   who knows
what old slavic way of thinking is this

"and i am saying this because i do not say that
every phonic grouping mirrors some aspect of the world or
even any   this of course is ridiculous   what i say is
this   in all the languages of the world are left some of
these original significant sound clusters that automatically
to us suggest certain meanings for which we have no words
because they are too deep for words

        "to these concrete original sounds i have given the
name   'submorphemic sememes'"

        at this point i would have interrupted with
powerful objections or at least with difficult questions
    but nasi was in full career and he waved his hand to
silence me and continued

        "many of these have been lost by the sound changes
    which are the results of centuries of small variations
of sound validating language errors fashions and fads   this
 is the process of degradation to which all social
institutions are subject   but this is only half of story
    the popular half   the one they tell all the time
about the clocks running down   corrupting of governments
    but the other half of story   of recovery   winding up
of clocks   reforming of governments   invention and
discovery of order   this they do not speak of   and it is
 not so popular

        "sure   all of these thousands of years we have
been speaking and losing order from our speech   but from
same spiritual principles what gave us linguistic order   we
have been restoring this order
                            if for centuries we have been
losing connections in some parts of a language between sounds
 and meanings   in some other parts we have been regaining
 them
        so that as some words are emptied of their sound
 meanings by lautverschiebungen   old words that had already
lost their imagery   through further sound changes gain new
 imagery or regain older images   and this process of
recovery is probably what in all cases made the great sound
 shifts so orderly   creating out of chaos of random changes
the systematic order of the great changes described by grimm

    196

and brugmann and verner

but this side of the story   of the motivating
force for the order of these changes   is even missing from
accounts given to us by great linguists like grimm and
brugmann and verner because they failed to recognize the
spiritual need to reconnect sound and meaning   and in so
doing overlooked the submorphemic sememe"

somewhat overwhelmed by this but still not
convinced i said   "nasi can you give me any examples of
these submorphemic sememes"

"plenty" he said   "and in your own language
consider /gl/   i say this with vowel naturally because
it always comes before a vowel which colors it   though it
does not matter which vowel   but this is a complicated
business i will explain some other time   but /gl/ gives

glamour
glare
glance
glitter
glisten
gleam
gloom
glaze
gloss
glow
glimpse
glimmer
glint

i call this for lack of better description   the
sememe of visual manifestation"

"what about gland" i said

"david   i never said that every word and morpheme
with this cluster is a sememe   some are preserved some are
annulled   some the results of accidents and will change
again   still may be that in the latin 'glandulus' or
'little acorn'   which this comes from is something of this
same making visible that might also be in 'globe'   from

197

latin 'globus'   as in the making round and therefore a prominence
           there is much here that i have still to understand
and i will check the celtic cognates   but consider /pl/

         pleasure
         pluck
         plough

   is filled with eroticism   and he went through dozens
of words with me in ten or eleven languages   and when i
would say   "plant   that doesnt sound very erotic to me"
      nasi would answer something like
                          "david how could you say
this   didnt you read erasmus darwin   he wrote a whole
book on the loves of the plants"
                     and i had to admit that
erasmus darwin had in fact written "the loves of the
plants"

      "you see"   said nasi   "/pl/ is filled with
eroticism   'plunge'   right away an erotic word   almost
  embarrasses me to say it   and there are many others"

         as it turned out   very many others   because nasi
  had collected hundreds or rather thousands of candidates
  for submorphemic sememe status in the thirty or forty
  languages he had been examining for this purpose for many
  years

         "but what are you going to do with them nasi?"   i
asked   because i was somewhat perplexed about the purpose of
  this great ongoing study

         "do?   i am doing it" he answered   "i am
collecting and studying all the possible submorphemic sememes
  from all the languages of the world   the ones that i know
and many that i do not know   i am studying them and testing
  them to see if they really are so   and i am doing this
  scientifically and structurally
         but because i do not wish to persuade by mere
rhetoric   merely to convince the minds and not the hearts
   i do not publish technical articles in the professional
journals   because as we all know   nothing is easier than

   198

to construct technical articles on any side of a scientific
  problem and all of them will sound plausible and none will
be conclusive   because science in the highest form must
  always become art
            so i am constructing from these submorphemic
sememes and from these sememes alone an epic poem   and this
  poem you will hear and understand   and there you will have
  the proof in the heart and not just the head   which this
is incontrovertible   and when i have this proof all worked
out i will print up copies of the poem on alexander godes
  printing press and there will be once and for all   for all
  the world to see and to hear   the complete list of all
these fundamental acoustical meaning clusters that made and
  make language possible among men   thus pronouncing the
name of the divine in man   which is language itself"

            "well nasi" i said   "are you going to give a
  reading of this poem?"

            "reading?   readings!   poetry readings?
    everybody gives public readings   public is for pigs"
he said   "pig sales you hold in public   not poetry
    poetry you must recite intimately   for friends lovers
  colleagues comrades   for this you dont hold readings
    poetry is no democracy   and what is democracy" he
  said   "there is no democracy of the spirit   there is
maybe brotherhood   universal brotherhood   this is maybe
  possible   but there is no democracy
            there is fraternité but no democrary   liberté may
also be   fraternité   but egalité?   what egalité?
    there is at best fraternité but no egalité   who knows
from egalité   we are equal only in the eyes of god" he
  said   "not to each other"

            "i speak twenty-five languages   he speaks nothing
    how much can he have inside him   not too much" he said
  "you david speak seven   thats almost as much"

            so what could i say   i said nasi when could you
give us   some of us   a private soirée-like reading?

            "dont say reading" he shouted   "say recitation"

            i said recitation

                                                    199

he said "yes recitation   like norwid like
mallarmé   a recitation" he said   "but only for a few
    you must arrange it david"

        i will arrange it i said   but youll have to tell
me who to invite

        "you will know" he said   "i leave that to you david
    you know spiritual people   only spiritual people
    they must be people of spirit who will not snicker or
laugh at spiritual things   many of which they may not
understand   many people are embarrassed in the presence of
    the divine   so they snicker and laugh and it escapes from
them   i am very serious and i know you are serious too
    you like to laugh often but   at the bottom you are a
serious person   i know   i can tell you are serious and
seriousness is the antechamber of the divine"

        "i'll do my best" i said
                                and i arranged a very
select audience   of about twenty people   some poets and
    painters and sculptors   and a handful of linguists and
    translators i thought would put up with the reading of one
very long poem   all friends from one part of nasis life or
another

        when we arrived   around eight oclock   yen lü
    led us through the anteroom   she was resplendently dressed
in a skin tight maroon sheath in which she could move only
because of a side slit that reached to her lower thigh
    with dark red heels and a pair of heavy iron earrings
    she was cool as always and led us silently into the main
room that had been darkened by drawing all the curtains and
was now illuminated by the light of candles in sconces fixed
to the columns that supported the roof   about thirty velvet
cushions were laid out on the floor around a raised central
    platform draped in black cloth on which nasi had set out
two candles a chinese vase with flowers and a large pile of
old black notebooks   of which i counted twenty-two as my
heart sank

        at 8:30 yen lü closed the door to the front room
and sat down on the platform facing the audience   nasi came

in wearing an improbable black suit with a white shirt and
string tie   went behind the table and nodding once to
acknowledge the audience and once to yen lü   he picked up
a notebook and without a word of introduction started to read

      he started to read in a low voice   and what he
read sounded at first like something you might overhear in an
open telephone booth in izmir or liubliana   a softly
urging voice speaking in a language vaguely familiar but not
quite comprehensible
                    this seemed to be some kind of
invocation because when it was over nasi's voice grew louder
and more animated   he began to read now in a droning
intonation that at times approached some kind of nasal
songlike quality and at others a kind of vigorous chanted
declamation   but it was not a language   it had too much
sound for that   it had a whole rainbow of sounds
      marvellous harsh clotted consonant clusters like
makhyedvezdjehrokshtchedras   or mbzoegvhwilkdringzyoents
      and an array of consonant sounds i had never heard in
any single language   velarized aspirated stops   dark and
clear /l/s   both voiced and voiceless   glottals and
pharyngeals i knew only from arabic and clicks i knew of
only from imbiri   while the array of vowels and diphthongs
was pure fireworks

      after about 15 minutes i looked around at the
audience to see how they were taking it   i caught a glimpse
of barbara holland   a fierce faced poet with a taste for
pentagrams spells and incantations   she seemed even paler
than usual and was following nasi with narrowed eyes   not
having a chair to hold onto she was holding her arms around
her knees resting her chin on them and following nasis every
move with the intensity of a rival magician   i looked
around and found howard ant   he was the poet lawyer who had
started up the readings at the old tenth street coffee shop
with mickey ruskin   he seemed to have found something
droll in one passage and had turned to his girl friend mary
and was grinning wickedly   paul blackburn was lying back
head on his hands supported by his pillow his galician wine
flask lying by his side and smiling sweetly up at the ceiling
listening dreamily   the abstract expressionist painter

with the wild hair and old testament face had his eyes
closed but was listening also
                              probably for some message from
   the desert   as i was listening too
                              because you could make
out phrases   often repeated or partially repeated   and
   pregnant pauses marked by pitch suspensions and sometimes
   rhymes   of consonants or vowels   and sometimes there
   were different voices that spoke in different styles   a
harsh voice very guttural and resonant   a whiney little
voice that spoke quite plaintively   or sometimes delicately
   in refined and mincing sounds   and there was another one
that was practically a roar   so that it was possible   out
   of this turbulent sea of sound   i thought in spite of the
   improbability   to pick out islands or even archipelagoes
of sense   at least to the extent that i began to
distinguish figures   i would even call them personages

          they had names   by which nasi from time to time
addressed them   sometimes preceded by what seemed
   honorifics like pan or gospodyin or herr   though i was not
always sure whether one personage was one or two   that is
   one personage with two aspects or two closely related
   figures   maybe twins   whose names were antafon and
   antifina   there was another   vaerunov   who was always
addressed with honorifics   and if he spoke it was in a dark
   voice filled with lower back vowels bounded by sonorants and
gutturals   the third   if it was the third and not the
   fourth   had a name something like tschaepueltapehk   and
the fifth was called oerterek

          now whenever antafon or antifina appeared   either
   just before or just afterward   we were in a lyrical
environment of soft or rippling sounds   something like

          soeffelen tcherreben   aemilef proeh
          oerefoel noedesh   soemisoel shwoeh
          toerrel toerrel soeffleshen thehn   oerefoel
          boerder noedesh shwoeh

   or

          khremereng proebra ekhera prehen

   202

nissela soerb   belemit oerb
balafaeng rafalter   tchesseren taer

and so on till they appeared   usually singly   either
antafon or antifina
but it wasnt long after a passage with
one of them that the other would come on the scene sometimes
with wailing sounds mournful nasals or /w/ sounds keening
like some desolate wind   which i figured must suggest their
separation and misery   and i tried to keep an eye on it
and measure how far apart they were by trying to calculate
how long it took to get from one to the other   but this was
a little hard to do because i wasnt sure how far back before
the name   say antafon   counted for his environment and
how much after   before antifina was announced   and it
was hard to keep track of anyway because there was so much
else going on   and someone else like vaehronov might
appear with a sound like the bassoons out of monteverdis
coronation of poppaea   and of course there was this
horrific roar whenever tschaepueltapaek came on the scene
that broke up everything around it

HOERRKHOHERR RHAAKHNARG HOERRKHOHERR
ARGHNARGHNARRAH

so i came to the conclusion that he was either a
dragon or a factory   and when you heard it advancing on
antafon or antifina

tschaepueltapehk kraezile seceedyed
vedyeed vedyeed vedyeed vedyeed vedyeedha

they would suddenly flee

deberen antifina ptsii ptsii ptsii ptsii

until they reached some sort of refuge or the flight was
interrupted by vaehronov coming on the scene

deberen khodjhiil dovertchiz vahrunov

his name seemed to undergo vowel changes in different
actions and environments   and then there would follow
moments of great solemnity and calm   as though he was
capable of dismissing the terrible threat of the dangerous

tschaepultapehkh   though he seemed to dismiss along with
him   it   antafon or antifina   who appeared to flee
from him as well   sometimes into a suppurating and slimy
  environment apparently inhabited by the sinuous oerterek
    who had nearly entrapped antafon   till somehow he was
liberated   barely   by antifina   at the price of
  becoming ensnared herself   or at least so it seemed to me
  several hours later when i had penetrated to the center of
the discourse   that was otherwise surrounded or encumbered
by great barriers   long passages of to me unintelligible
  sound

        but the entire audience stayed with nasi through
    the clotted verbal forest of his poem late into the night
      and some time in the early morning after vaehrunov had
made his final appearance   reducing the apparently
destroyed world of his poem   the murdered souls of antafon
and antifina   finally done in by the violence of
    tdschapueltapehks malice   and tdsschaepultapekh
      engulfed in the fatal swamp by the mortally wounded yet
wily oerterek   to a great calm   in which even vaehrunov
disappeared   that lasted for nearly half an hour   nasi
  with a sudden
              GRRRAACK
                        closed his notebook kissed the hand
of yen lü   genya   blew out the candles and bowed to us
    and i realized that the recitation if not the poem was
over

        the next day i saw nasi at an opening   "you see
david you understood   i saw you smiling when the poem was
gay   groaning when it was terrible   grimacing when it was
  grotesque   so were your friends   so it is revealed
    there is divinity in people   and it is the universals
of language   this is proved by my poem   which is not even
finished
        and when this work is complete and finally published
    you will see how through my additions to the *principes
de phonologie* of prince troubetzkoy   you will be
illuminated   because i am sure that there were many
  passages of my poem that were obscure to you   so were
they to me   and i will also be illuminated   because you

must not imagine that as they were dark to you they were not
also dark to me" he said   "because they were dark passages
     and this is what means a study   for what is there to
study where everything is light?
                                        for partial darkness is the
condition of all regular works of art   like poems like
paintings   in which the artist never knows what they mean
  until he has made them and not even then   because art is
like speech is a gift from the god who is only making himself
  available to us bit by bit in the work   and like everyone
else i will understand only later   when the work is
complete and i have had time to reflect on the divinity that
  was given to me"

          then we went about our business   drinking or
talking or working or going off to another opening or party
     and i would see nasi from time to time   we would run
  into each other occasionally in the art world or the
translating world   and i would ask him how his work was
  coming   and it was always progressing   the paintings and
  the poem   he had filled nearly forty notebooks now

          sometimes i'd run into someone who'd been at the
recitation who didnt make either of nasis two scenes   the
art scene or the translating scene   and theyd ask me about
nasi

          "whats become of that little man?" barbara holland
asked me   "that muscular little man with the terrible poem
about witchcraft and sorcery?"   about nine months later i
ran into paul blackburn   he was organizing some reading for
a bookstore over on the east side and he asked whatever
happened to nasi   whether he'd ever done anything with
  that long funny poem he was writing and whether i thought
he might like to do another reading from it   but i didnt
know   because nasi had dropped completely out of sight   i
hadnt seen him for a long time at any of his favorite haunts
    it had been months since i'd run into him at a gallery
or loft or at a translating agency   i'd checked out the
waldorf without success   and none of the language regulars
there could remember having seen him for weeks   then i ran
  into him one day coming out of the subway near union square

and he was looking remarkably seedy   pale and unshaven
and very dejected

i said nasi how are you   where have you been
how is the work?

"terrible" he said   "terrible   i have come to a
complete stall"

and i looked at this once cheerful drinking dancing
dwarf and he looked hardly a shadow of his former self

"what do you mean nasi?"

he said "my poem has come to a complete stall
breakdown collapse   phhht" he said snapping his
fingers   "i am finished kaputt"

"how come?"

he said   "genya has left me"

i said "nasi i'm very sorry but what happened?"

"she ran off with the heavy metal sculptor   the
dumb one   he is not fit to carry out her garbage   but
what is that   she ran off with him"   i said well its
too bad but all great artists suffer setbacks   its part of
the tradition

"but she was my muse" he said "my muse   only she
could evoke from me the divinity that was put in my mouth to
speak and to write"

i said maybe she could still come around and visit
like a model   she could come in and listen a few hours a
day

he said "david dont even say such a thing   it
pains me   i cry to think of this   how could you say such
a thing i cannot look on her face again"   kssst   he spat
and shook his head violently   "it is terrible to talk this
way   please do not try to comfort me   i am inconsolable
a husk a shell   i am extinguished like a cigarette stub
the fire has gone out   the vessel of the godhead has
been broken and lies in fragments at my feet   forty-two
notebooks   and it will not be finished"

206

i said   maybe you should publish it the way it is
as a work in progress   and later maybe you   could bring it
to completion   besides forty-two notebooks is a lot of
 printing   itll take a long time to publish them   and by
then who knows   you could find the energy again

     he said "david i am too depressed to even cry
 lets go get something to eat"

     and then i lost track of him for another year or so
     and he died   he wasnt a young man   he drank a lot
and i suppose his heart was bad   in any case he died   and
the next time i saw him was at his funeral where they had an
 open coffin and a lot of flowers   and lying there with
his hands crossed and his beard combed   and with the
undertakers coloring he looked almost his old self again

     there were not too many people there   he had no
relatives   just a few artists translators and linguists
     the metal sculptor and genya   looking dark and
beautiful   she must have made the arrangements   there
was a short service by a heavily bearded man   one of the
 linguists spoke   and it was all over
                                             of the paintings and
 the notebooks   i gathered that according to the will
     along with all of nasis prized possessions   his
library his greek typewriter   they had been left to genya
     who broke up with the metal sculptor and seems to have
disappeared   because nobody i knew ever saw her again
     apparently she never approached a publisher with the
notebooks   or any of the galleries with the paintings
     which werent very fashionable anyway

     so this extraordinary epic poem   written in no
known language by my structuralist friend never saw the light
 of day   and the truth of the divinity of language and its
universal constituents   revealed through the speech of
this man as evoked by the beauty and sympathy of that woman
 will probably remain obscure to us forever

New Directions Paperbooks—A Partial Listing

Walter Abish, *How German Is It.* NDP508.
John Allman, *Scenarios for a Mixed Landscape.*
NDP619.
Wayne Andrews, *The Surrealist Parade.* NDP689.
David Antin, *Tuning.* NDP570.
G. Apollinaire, *Selected Writings.*† NDP310.
Jimmy S. Baca, *Martín & Meditations.* NDP648.
Black Mesa Poems. NDP676.
Djuna Barnes, *Nightwood.* NDP98.
J. Barzun, *An Essay on French Verse.* NDP708.
H.E. Bates, *Elephant's Nest in a Rhubarb Tree.* NDP669.
A Party for the Girls, NDP653.
Charles Baudelaire, *Flowers of Evil.*† NDP684.
Paris Spleen. NDP294.
Bei Dao, *Old Snow.* NDP727.
Waves. NDP693.
Gottfried Benn, *Primal Vision.* NDP322.
Carmel Bird, *The Bluebird Café.* NDP707.
R. P. Blackmur, *Studies in Henry James,* NDP552.
Wolfgang Borchert, *The Man Outside.* NDP319.
Jorge Luis Borges, *Labyrinths.* NDP186.
Seven Nights. NDP576.
Kay Boyle, *Life Being the Best.* NDP654.
Three Short Novels. NDP703.
Buddha, *The Dhammapada.* NDP188.
M. Bulgakov, *Flight & Bliss.* NDP593.
The Life of M. de Moliere. NDP601.
Frederick Busch, *Absent Friends.* NDP721.
Veza Canetti, *Yellow Street.* NDP709.
Ernesto Cardenal, *Zero Hour.* NDP502.
Joyce Cary, *A House of Children.* NDP631.
Mister Johnson. NDP631.
Hayden Carruth, *Tell Me Again. . . .* NDP677.
Louis-Ferdinand Céline,
Death on the Installment Plan. NDP330.
Journey to the End of the Night. NDP542.
René Char. *Selected Poems.*† NDP734.
Jean Cocteau, *The Holy Terrors.* NDP212.
M. Collis, *She Was a Queen.* NDP716.
Cid Corman, *Sun Rock Man.* NDP318.
Gregory Corso, *Long Live Man.* NDP127.
Herald of the Autochthonic Spirit. NDP522.
Robert Creeley, *Memory Gardens.* NDP613.
Windows. NDP687.
Edward Dahlberg, *Because I Was Flesh.* NDP227.
Alain Daniélou, *The Way to the Labyrinth.* NDP634.
Osamu Dazai, *The Setting Sun.* NDP258.
No Longer Human. NDP357.
Mme. de Lafayette, *The Princess of Cleves.* NDP660.
E. Dujardin, *We'll to the Woods No More.* NDP682.
Robert Duncan, *Ground Work.* NDP571.
Ground Work II: In the Dark. NDP647.
Richard Eberhart, *The Long Reach.* NDP565.
Wm. Empson, *7 Types of Ambiguity.* NDP204.
Some Versions of Pastoral. NDP92.
S. Endo, *Stained Glass Elegies.* NDP699.
Wm. Everson, *The Residual Years.* NDP263.
Gavin Ewart, *Selected Poems.* NDP655
Lawrence Ferlinghetti, *Endless Life.* NDP516.
A Coney Island of the Mind. NDP74.
European Poems & Transitions. NDP582
Starting from San Francisco. NDP220.
Wild Dreams of a New Beginning. NDP663.
Ronald Firbank, *Five Novels.* NDP581.
Three More Novels. NDP614.
F. Scott Fitzgerald, *The Crack-up.* NDP54.
Gustave Flaubert, *Dictionary.* NDP230.
J. Gahagan, *Did Gustav Mahler Ski?* NDP711.
Gandhi, *Gandhi on Non-Violence.* NDP197.
Gary, Romain, *Promise at Dawn.* NDP635.
The Life Before Us ("Madame Rosa"). NDP604.
W. Gerhardie, *Futility.* NDP722.
Goethe, *Faust,* Part I. NDP70.
Henry Green, *Back.* NDP517
Allen Grossman, *The Ether Dome.* NDP723.
Martin Grzimek, *Shadowlife.* NDP705.
Guignonat, Henri, *Daemon in Lithuania.* NDP592.
Lars Gustafsson, *The Death of a Beekeeper.* NDP523.
Stories of Happy People. NDP616.

John Hawkes, *The Beetle Leg.* NDP239.
Humors of Blood & Skin. NDP577.
Second Skin. NDP146.
Samuel Hazo, *To Paris.* NDP512.
H. D. *Collected Poems.* NDP611.
The Gift. NDP546.
Helen in Egypt. NDP380.
HERmione. NDP526.
Selected Poems. NDP658.
Tribute to Freud. NDP572.
Robert E. Helbling, *Heinrich von Kleist.* NDP390.
William Herrick, *Love and Terror.* NDP538.
Herman Hesse, *Siddhartha.* NDP65.
Paul Hoover, *The Novel.* NDP706.
Vicente Huidobro, *Selected Poetry.* NDP520.
C. Isherwood, *All the Conspirators.* NDP480.
The Berlin Stories. NDP134.
Ledo Ivo, *Snake's Nest.* NDP521.
Gustav Janouch, *Conversations with Kafka.* NDP313.
Alfred Jarry, *Ubu Roi.* NDP105.
Robinson Jeffers, *Cawdor and Medea.* NDP293.
B.S. Johnson, *Christie Malry's. . . .* NDP600.
Albert Angelo. NDP628.
James Joyce, *Stephen Hero.* NDP133.
Franz Kafka, *Amerika.* NDP117.
Bob Kaufman, *The Ancient Rain.* NDP514.
H. von Kleist, *Prince Friedrich.* NDP462.
Shimpei Kusano, *Asking Myself. . . .* NDP566.
Jules Laforgue, *Moral Tales.* NDP594.
P. Lal, *Great Sanskrit Plays.* NDP142.
Tommaso Landolfi, *Gogol's Wife.* NDP155.
"Language" Poetries: An Anthology. NDP630.
D. Larsen, *Stitching Porcelain.* NDP710.
Lautréamont, *Maldoror.* NDP207.
Irving Layton, *Selected Poems.* NDP431.
Christine Lehner, *Expecting.* NDP544.
H. Leibowitz, *Fabricating Lives.* NDP715.
Siegfried Lenz, *The German Lesson.* NDP618.
Denise Levertov, *Breathing the Water.* NDP640.
Candles in Babylon. NDP533.
A Door in the Hive. NDP685.
Poems 1960-1967. NDP549.
Poems 1968-1972. NDP629.
Oblique Prayers. NDP578.
Harry Levin, *James Joyce.* NDP87.
Li Ch'ing-chao, *Complete Poems.* NDP492.
Enrique Lihn, *The Dark Room.*† NDP542.
C. Lispector, *Soulstorm.* NDP671.
The Hour of the Star. NDP733.
Garciá Lorca, *Five Plays.* NDP232
The Public & Play Without a Title. NDP561.
Selected Poems.† NDP114
Three Tragedies. NDP52.
Francisco G. Lorca, *In The Green Morning.* NDP610.
Michael McClure, *Rebel Lions.* NDP712.
Selected Poems. NDP599.
Carson McCullers, *The Member of the
Wedding.* (Playscript) NDP153.
Stéphane Mallarme,† *Selected Poetry and
Prose.* NDP529.
Thomas Merton, *Asian Journal.* NDP394.
New Seeds of Contemplation. ND337.
Selected Poems. NDP85.
Thomas Merton in Alaska. NDP652.
The Way of Chuang Tzu. NDP276.
The Wisdom of the Desert. NDP295.
Zen and the Birds of Appetite. NDP261.
Henri Michaux, *A Barbarian in Asia.* NDP622.
Selected Writings. NDP264.
Henry Miller, *The Air-Conditioned Nightmare.*
NDP302.
Big Sur & The Oranges. NDP161.
The Colossus of Maroussi. NDP75.
Into the Heart of Life. NDP728.
The Smile at the Foot of the Ladder. NDP386.
Stand Still Like the Hummingbird. NDP236.
The Time of the Assassins. NDP115.
Y. Mishima, *Confessions of a Mask.* NDP253.
Death in Midsummer. NDP215.

For complete listing request free catalog from
New Directions, 80 Eighth Avenue, New York 10011

†Bilingual

For complete listing request free catalog from
New Directions, 80 Eighth Avenue, New York 10011   †Bilingual